Crazy Age

Also by Jane Miller

Many Voices: Bilingualism, Culture and Education
Women Writing about Men
Seductions: Studies in Reading and Culture
More Has Meant Women: The Feminisation of Schooling
School for Women
Relations

Crazy Age

Thoughts on Being Old

JANE MILLER

virago

VIRAGO

First published in Great Britain in 2010 by Virago Press

Copyright © Jane Miller 2010

The moral right of the author has been asserted.

A CIP catalogue record for this book
is available from the British Library.

ISBN 978-1-84408-649-8

Typeset in Perpetua by M Rules
Printed and bound in Great Britain by
Clays Ltd, St Ives plc

Papers used by Virago are natural, renewable and
recyclable products sourced from well-managed forests and certified
in accordance with the rules of the Forest Stewardship Council.

Mixed Sources
Product group from well-managed
forests and other controlled sources
www.fsc.org   Cert no. SGS-COC-004081
© 1996 Forest Stewardship Council
FSC

Virago Press
An imprint of
Little, Brown Book Group
100 Victoria Embankment
London EC4Y 0DY

An Hachette UK Company
www.hachette.co.uk

www.virago.co.uk

To Natasha, Roxana, Tara, Zubin, Dora
and Joseph, with love

Contents

1

Crazy Age

I am old and I feel and look old. In addition, I think about being old a good deal of the time; not crossly or sadly, as a rule, but simply as a condition of my days and nights and what's going on in them. I like being old at least as much as I liked being middle-aged and a good deal more than I liked being young. There are lots of bad things about it, but then there were lots of bad things about being young. There must have been, since my favourite poems were for a time John Clare's 'Written in Northampton County Asylum', which starts with the line 'I am, yet what I am who cares, or knows?' and a poem by the Russian poet Lermontov called, roughly, 'It's Boring and Sad and Lonely'. Lermontov died in a duel when he was twenty-seven, and a good deal of what he wrote was about the loneliness and emptiness of life and its all being a bad joke, so I wonder whether he mightn't have rather preferred being old. Needless to say, I can hardly bear to read either poem through to the end these days. I'm not keen on hearing about people having a mouldy time of it, and especially not young people; which cuts out a good deal of Romantic poetry. All that pain and longing looks different from here. Though I'm not sure that the suicide statistics bear me out. It seems that the highest number of suicides in this country has for years been among men of over seventy-five and then (though there are far fewer of these) among women of the same age.

On the whole I take pleasure in my life and am not especially anxious for it to end, despite reminders from all quarters that the end is nigh for us all and even hints that it might sensibly be brought forward. But I've been lucky. I was born in 1932. I'm in my late seventies, and I still live with the person I married fifty-four years ago, whose work as a journal editor and academic has introduced us both to people who have, for most of the time, been lucky too. I have children and grandchildren; though one son has decided to live in India, rather than up the road. I have had interesting work to do throughout my life: publishing, teaching in a school and then a university, writing. All that has furnished friends, too. And I still know, despite the ravages of time and death, a good many people as old as I am, or older, and quite a few who are younger than me as well. My ninety-two-year-old aunt, who died recently, wore silvery eye-shadow to the day she died, and when she talked, as she did, about a possible end to her awful pain and her immobility, I don't think she meant dying. She wanted to get back to her work, which was teaching singers to sing, and she wanted to sit in her garden. She was pleased when I followed her bedizening example in my adolescence, and used to refer to herself as 'Auntie Jezebel'. I have several friends in their nineties and even more who are just a whisker away: most of them, as it happens, in full possession of their wits, and all of them weakened to some extent by their bodies' failures. Collectively, they are deaf, blind, severely breathless and arthritic. There have been broken hips and arms and pelvises, mismanaged cataract operations, glaucoma and recurring leg ulcers. There have been multiple bypasses and the insertion of stents. And, of course, cancer of several kinds and a stroke or two. And in each case there are anxious and by now fairly elderly offspring braced to insist on live-in help for them and to install warning systems, alterations to staircases, bathrooms and bedrooms and lavatories, and in some cases there has been covert investigation of care homes.

Most of these kindly suggestions are stubbornly rebuffed. And collectively, these nonagenarians fly around the world accepting prizes, playing bridge, swimming, reading books and even writing them. They work and see their friends and make jokes, and behave like inhabitants of a world they assume is going to continue with them in it. One of them admitted to me recently that this was probably not the happiest time of her life, but she still marvels at the beauty and charm of a world she can only dimly see, and given half a reason to dress up will do so with elegance and aplomb. These are people who know that they are likely to be dead within the next five years, and yet they give little sense of being haunted by death or dreading it, as do many people much younger than they are. It may even be that the sense of an imminent ending gives shape and urgency to the life they're living now. They live daily with their own mortality, and, as Bernard Williams the philosopher once wrote in an essay he subtitled 'Reflections on the Tedium of Immortality', 'death gives the meaning to life' – though, as he quickly added, 'That does not mean that we should not fear death'. It is possible that loneliness and boredom are balanced for the very old by the relief these states may provide from the speed and noise and some of the pain of other people's lives, though the old are by no means immune to the horrors of depression.

Ever since I have inhabited old age – for that is what it feels like – I have looked and listened, mostly in vain, for news of what it is like for other people who inhabit it as I do. Naturally, I'm interested in its well-known depredations, the physical and mental ones that people in their forties and fifties so publicly dread, and those other ones in the world out there, which cause us to throw up our hands in horror when people use words like 'digital' or 'leverage' or 'unacceptable' or 'inappropriate' or 'issues' or start a lot of their sentences with 'At the end of the day' and expect us to listen to what comes next. And who would not delight in all the theatrical props of old age: the pills and sticks, the shrieking hearing-aids and dental weaponry, the tricks for countering the loss of names and threads and glasses and for circumventing insomnia, the visits to The Back Shop? But that's not all. I have a fond hope that there may be new kinds of time and new kinds of pleasure, perhaps even new kinds of vitality, and that though we forget and muddle and fail to hear things, there may be moments when we understand what's going on for the first time. But then I've always been a late developer.

No doubt the old have delivered themselves of too much advice and opinion over the years and deserve to be asked to keep quiet now, but it does sometimes seem that we are hemmed in by unnecessary and even self-inflicted prohibitions. It is nearly forbidden to talk about age. I am always being warned off it, as a subject unseemly in itself and one which, once broached, is bound to end in complaints and sorrow. Helen Small, who has considered old age as a philosopher and as someone who is not yet old, has written that 'many of us spend more and more time, as we grow older, thinking about the fact that we are growing older and what it implies, but we also spend a great deal of time trying, more or less strenuously, *not* to think about that fact and what it implies'. Even Simone de Beauvoir, who wrote a book nearly seven hundred pages long about old age, ended it with the advice that 'it is far better not to think about it too much'. Wanderings down 'memory lane' produce polite interest, but little more. And you may simply be cut short by people's attempts at consolation, and embarrassed assurances (from those who are old themselves as well as from the young) that no one would guess how old you are, and that since you are probably young in heart and spirit, if nothing else, you should feel no shame or self-pity, nor dwell on the condition unduly. I suppose that we may seem to be asking for some such homily or reassurance, and some of us are. The mother of an old friend of mine used to ask absolute strangers at bus stops how old they thought she was. Her announcement, delivered before they could reply, that she was eighty-four, was clearly meant to elicit incredulity.

This embargo on old age as a topic reminds me of my early years as a mother, when we tried not to talk about our babies for fear of being thought boring; and the babies themselves were expected to remain as far as possible unseen and unheard. Perhaps we were pretending that someone else was looking after them. I remember a grand lady's indignation when a guest at her Sunday lunch brought a dog with her. 'One wouldn't, after all,' the grand lady announced later, 'bring one's baby!' Since having a baby was the most interesting thing that had happened to me so far it seemed surprising that one couldn't talk about it more. Some of all that may just have been squeamishness about bodies and their various leakages. Many years ago I fielded a telephone call to my husband from the writer V. S. Pritchett without mentioning to him that I was actually in labour, in mid-contraction. He would not, I felt, have wanted to know.

So why are there people who allow these extra years, after, say, sixty, to collapse into something like an awkward afterthought, a sort of terminal waiting-room or exile, where the earlier themes and continuities of our lives are to be treated as radically attenuated, altered or defunct? These extra years would have seemed a miraculous bonus to many of our forebears. We are not encouraged to dwell in the past, and in sticking to the present, we are warned off mimicking the young or over-identifying with them. We must guard against petulance about the modern world, while also insisting, if possible, that from our vantage point some things have changed for the better. I confess to occasional feelings of relief that I may not have to share the terrifying future predicted for us all by public doomsters warning of political, economic and environmental disasters. Meanwhile, we must keep off the subject of death while also preparing realistically and practically for its imminence, and we are to be sparing in our discussion of illness, pain and all signs of degeneration. These things are not, after all, a pretty sight.

I exaggerate, of course: for one of the charms of old age is that one has more time and space in which to think one's thoughts, if not always to utter them; and if I feel oppressed by these kinds of prohibition that is more likely to derive from my own history of distrusting the old than from some more general ordinance. For I did distrust them. I thought of old people as generally dowdy and disapproving, so that I was easily won over by my grandfather and a very few other old people, who seemed, for most of the time at least, to be neither.

Only the very young want to be older, and surely even they do not want to be very old. Does anyone? Probably not, though perhaps there are people who look forward to age, rather as Henry James looked forward to becoming stout. I see that there is really no reason for the young to bother themselves with old age or with the very old or even with wondering what it's going to be like. Being able to ignore the future and possible endings to it is what you're young for, after all. But why should the old feel bound to follow their example? Most of us are faced these days with the serious alternative of becoming old rather than ending our lives as so many did in the past (and still do in poor parts of the world) in their thirties or forties. Several of my friends have died in their thirties or forties. I think they missed the best bit and I am sad for them. Yet old age remains as unpopular as it ever was.

About twenty years ago I sat in a restaurant gazing at the left forearm of the American writer who was sitting opposite me. As she reminisced about Hollywood and a very public quarrel she'd had recently with another veteran writer, I marvelled at her arm. Adorned with gold rings and watch and bracelets, its sunburnt wrinkles were neat and regular, like the ripples left by the tide on a sandy beach. I imagined her whole body wrapped in more of this finely pleated, tissue-paper skin, and I hoped (and believed, I think) that it would never happen to me. Something very like it has happened to me, though I can flex my arms a bit and get them to return to a semblance of their old selves, just as I can pretend that my strange leopard's markings are simply freckles of an unusual kind. But there are ugly arthritic twists to my fingers and odd lumps where my thumbs begin. I don't wear rings any more, in order to avoid drawing attention to my hands. I am not horrified by these changes and not self-conscious about them, as I would have been when I was young. They have happened to me slowly, gradually, and I have forgotten what my arms were like before, though I scrutinise young arms with an astonished pleasure I don't remember feeling about my own limbs. I don't think that people of my age look at themselves in mirrors much. The person we occasionally glimpse there is someone else, with only a remote resemblance to the person we expected to see. Yet this unfamiliar mask we wear nowadays can be easier to live behind than that other face we had somehow to account for as it presented itself to the world. It was our fortune, after all, and this one isn't. I have no attachment to this new look: but its very foreignness affords solace, curiously, and I have no impulse to apologise for it or cover it up, even when, as happened recently, a two-year-old boy looked up from his scooter to ask me if I was a man. I suppose he wouldn't have asked if there hadn't been some chance of my not being.

Dora, my granddaughter, made a charming Romeo in her school play when she was twelve, though she was a little dwarfed by the tallest girl in her class, who had been lavishly greyed-up as the Nurse. When I was sixteen and was suddenly and punitively, as it seemed to me, sent to a school with no boys in it, I was chosen to play a sixty-year-old man in a play called *Quiet Weekend*. Bert, once wigmaker to stars of stage and screen, who'd been at school with my English teacher's brother, fitted me out with a bald head and gingery whiskers, while cushions were stuffed into my rather thin father's tweed jacket and grey flannels to persuade the audience that I was not only male but old. In those days, masquerading as an old person seemed easy enough. You knew the rules: you were bent and grey and stumbling and slow and you lowered your voice a bit. Apart from that it was a matter of make-up. There is a road sign encouraging drivers to look out for elderly pedestrians, which has it exactly:

two bent figures with sticks. I once asked a class of twelve-year-olds to write about their grandmothers, and there they all were: small, bent, shuffling, kindly, knitting away and putting logs on the fire. One even scratched her head with a knitting needle under her headscarf. Another did some fancy work removing her false teeth semi-invisibly behind a handkerchief. Only one had his grandmother stalking the Côte d'Azur in hotpants, downing the G and Ts provided by the sly young gigolos her grandson remembered admiring and even envying. We've played at being grown-up and we've impersonated the old. A trick of the light and the impersonation impersonates itself.

If impersonation and old age are not synonymous, they are certainly linked. There's the story of Harold Macmillan and Rab Butler making their rivalrous way in a funeral procession at Westminster Abbey: Macmillan all sticks and aids and senile pantomime. 'It's all put on, you know,' Butler is said to have whispered loudly to his neighbour. The selves we present to the world can seem like disguises to us – histrionic disguises that are usually taken to be the real thing. While the young may think that we have always been as we are now, most of us continue to see ourselves at our optimum age. In her nineties, my mother drew and painted herself, in scenes with her great-grandchildren, as a woman of forty or so. Most of my memories of people who were old in my childhood and youth are curiously fixed, unchanging, cast as the permanent furniture of my memory, and quite independently of their lives and times. In some cases, however, I have a single additional memory. It is of their sudden falling away, becoming ill, collapsed, about to die. I remember my grandfather, just before he took to his bed and died of a brain tumour, sitting slumped and weak, as he had never seemed before, on the shallow wooden steps in his library. At eighty-one, he was suddenly defeated by the woman who was visiting him in order to collaborate on a book about the Irish potato famine, a subject he knew more about at that moment than anyone else in the world. She, I have always supposed, took comfort from his disintegration, and wrote the book they'd planned together without him and without even acknowledging his help. I remember the shock I felt at his helplessness, a condition that was alien to everything I knew of him.

Some people have surgery and go to other lengths to freeze themselves in youth or, more uncomfortably, to freeze themselves in those years that follow immediately after youth, when the beginnings of ageing are already visible. One woman I know looks younger and prettier in her seventies than I remember her in her twenties, as a result of some quite elaborate surgery I believe she is happy to admit to. She is one of several of my contemporaries who have become much younger than I am, as a result of plastic surgery or lying about their age, or both, or perhaps because they really are younger than I am in spirit. When the old are the subject of magazine articles it is often because they are famous and look much younger than they are. It is as if not seeming old is the main achievement the old may decently aspire to. An Indian friend explained to me that not dying your hair could be thought antisocial, bad manners, unfair on one's friends. She encourages the men in her family to dye their hair too. I am surprised by the passion with which some people strive to hold on to their youth or to reclaim it. I wonder if they enjoyed their youth more than I did, or if they didn't have enough of it, or not enough of a good time when they were young. And I am moved by that moment when people in their fifties begin to look older and struggle for the first time with the signs of age and with a sense of their own mortality and deterioration. I remember that moment as far harder to bear than the transformation and the invisibility I live with now.

While thinking about the disadvantages of immortality, Bernard Williams wondered especially about the age we'd choose to stick at for immortal life, for eternity, if we assume that we wouldn't just go on getting older and older: 'If one pictures living for ever as living as an embodied person in the world rather as it is, it will be a question, and not so trivial as may seem, of what age one eternally is.' Forty-two seemed about right to Williams. To be eternally in one's seventies might have considerably less appeal. I wonder how many of us are old in our dreams. I have the sense that if we figure at all in our rehearsals and imaginings and memories, we are either invisible ghostly presences there or much, much younger. I dreamed some nights ago that I cheated in a maths exam, a strange feat for me, as it meant copying a long and inscrutable formula from some secret source. I assume I was young in my dream, but perhaps my cheating stood in for some riper crime, committed in old age. If we 'let ourselves go', as they say, isn't it because these selves we are required to maintain and adorn and keep going do not always seem to us to be our true selves, but belatedly imposed or adopted selves, even provisional ones, so that it is sometimes quite difficult to be interested in them? Making the best of what is, after all, quite a bad job, simply stops being worth it. No wonder that shopping and dressing and washing and brushing and combing become a bit dull and perfunctory.

In his *Nothing to Be Frightened Of*, a meditation on his lifelong fear of dying, Julian Barnes divides people into those who fear death and those who fear the incapacities of old age, with subheadings for those who do or don't believe in God or an afterlife. (There must surely be a superordinate category containing those who fear both.) 'I'm sure my father feared death, and fairly certain my mother didn't: she feared incapacity and dependence more,' Barnes writes, aligning himself with his father and placing his older, philosopher brother firmly alongside his mother, while, perhaps a bit disingenuously, affecting to believe in the superiority of those who would put themselves in his mother's camp. But I don't think there's much question of his real position: 'my fear of death has become an essential part of me, and I would attribute it to the exercise of the imagination; while my brother's detachment in death's face is an essential part of him, which he probably ascribes to the exercise of logical thought.' If it is indeed to be a battle to the death between imagination and logical thought, I would have to hitch a ride with the unimaginative. I don't think about death very much, or anyway not about my own. I do deeply and constantly fear the death of several other people, probably because other people's deaths, their dying and their being dead, have always been easier to imagine than my own. In fact, I don't think much about my own death or even fear it, I suppose because I am unable to imagine it. How can I imagine myself being unable to imagine myself? But I did catch myself hoping the other day that I might have most of my teeth when I'm dying, if only to spare the sensibility of an onlooker, should there be one. It is a hope all too likely to be thwarted, I'm sorry to say.

If I have no hopes or plans for an afterlife, I do, clearly, have some thought for posterity. And I hate to think that my grandchildren may be obliged to remember me as 'sans teeth, sans eyes, sans taste, sans everything'. Vanity, no doubt of that. But my absence from my own death and my own funeral robs both of a good deal of interest. My funeral is not, after all, a family occasion I shall be required to organise. And what will be the point of it, anyway, if I'm not at it and not therefore in a position to check who is and who is not?

I can imagine all too easily, on the other hand, the stretch of life preceding death, and its potential for misery, weakness, dependence, though I don't think about that very much either, probably because I can't bear to. I am terrified of having nothing to do and no one to talk to. I avoid all articles and programmes advising me to insure myself now for dementia and other debilities, book a place in a home or negotiate a granny flat, let alone join EXIT or look into the fees, legality and conditions of death-delivering doctors in Switzerland. We can pretty well count on a nasty future, but there's no need to cover all the possibilities or spend time on it quite yet. The only thing I learned from the longish periods of incapacity suffered by both my parents before they died was that there was no point in planning ahead, because everything could change in a day, and did, and people are as different from each other when they are ill and dying as they ever were. When Simon Gray was told that his lung cancer would kill him, he and his wife decided not to ask for an exact prognosis or timetable, though they were given one anyway. So that the last book he wrote, *Coda*, which follows the three 'Smoking Diaries' – marvellously funny accounts of getting old – is about a year spent dying in the shadow of a doctor's unasked for and unwelcome prognosis, which fulfils itself with grim precision.

Montaigne thought it madness 'to expect to die of that failing of our powers brought on by extreme old age . . . Dying of old age is a rare death, unique and out of the normal order and therefore less natural than the others.' He was fifty-nine, in fact, when he died, a challenge by the standard of the times to his own prediction, though an obituary today would probably describe such a death as happening too tragically soon to allow for the proper or complete fulfilment of his promise.

I should come clean. I'm not sure that I really believe that I will be dead one day, any more than I entirely believe that I'm as old as I am. Somewhere, in some part of me, I am still young and possibly eternal. I wonder whether most of us feel that in essence we are still young, and that the problem with old age is precisely that it comes to define us, blotting out earlier versions of ourselves, standing in for them, taking over. David Rieff, writing about his mother Susan Sontag and her refusal to accept illness and death, says that she 'came to being ill imbued with a profound sense of being the exception to every rule . . . On a certain level, all modern people who are not utterly beaten down by experience early and whose good fortune is that their tragedies come later in life feel this way.'

I would like to think that everyone has moments when they think of themselves as the exception to the rule, though most people are discouraged from doing so either by religion or common sense. Writing about my own old age is a way of convincing myself that I really am old and that I really will die. Old age has not meant that I have given up on either rage or anxiety, which suggests that I am by no means reconciled to endings or anything else. I still burn with both emotions, and anxiety has become perpetual, though more various with time. I think of fear and worry as constant conditions, though both are capable of peaking almost uncontrollably at times, beyond their normal Plimsoll line. My heart races and thumps, just as it's said to, at absurdly trivial misfortunes: the least hint of things going wrong with my car, for instance, or with the heating or the washing-machine. But in addition, I imagine the worst things that could happen to my family and friends and sometimes, though less often, to myself. And I imagine them in minute

detail. I try to think of these panics and imaginings as ther-
apeutic, as providing magic protection from their happening
in reality, and I hope they do.

Most of the clichés about old age are contradictory, as they
need to be. There are people who see it as a time of peace,
acceptance and the end of strong feeling. One of Alice
Munro's characters wonders whether she might be transformed by age. 'She has seen the look on the faces of certain
old people – marooned on islands of their own choosing,
clear-sighted, content.' I do know old people who seem to
have reached a plateau of that sort. They are amused, interested, calm, and they appear to have accepted the
inevitability of their distance from a great deal of what goes
on in the world, though I suspect that they are often secretly
irritated by other people's assumption of that distance,
indeed reliance on it. Yet in their desire both to live a good
old age and to control the manner of their dying I doubt
whether many of them would go quite as far as the old or ill
adherents of Jainism in India sometimes do. William
Dalrymple talked to a nun about the Jain custom of gently
starving yourself to death, a process she firmly distinguishes
from suicide:

> *sallekhana* is a beautiful thing. There is no distress or cru-
> elty. As nuns our lives are peaceful, and giving up the
> body should also be peaceful . . . First you fast one day a
> week, then you eat only on alternate days: one day you
> take food, the next you fast. One by one, you give up

different types of foodstuffs. You give up rice, then fruits, then vegetables, then juice, then buttermilk. Finally you take only water, and then you have that only on alternate days. Eventually, when you are ready, you give up on that too. If you do it very gradually, there is no suffering at all. The body is cooled down, so that you can concentrate inside on the soul and on erasing all your bad karma.

There is an entirely different version of old age: the old person who is angry, impatient, full of regrets, nostalgia, distrust of the young; and there's a particular bitterness and resentment such a person may go in for, stored up from the past and sharpened now by powerlessness and by embarrassing and ineffectual efforts to garner and maintain dignity. Dylan Thomas was thirty-seven when he wrote 'Do Not Go Gentle into That Good Night' with its injunction that 'Old age should burn and rave at close of day.' It was advice I approved of in those days, even though the poor fellow died two years later, when he was not yet forty. It would be hard for most of us to keep up all that burning and raving in our seventies. When the poet Rochester's young lady praises her elderly lover for not yet being 'Aking, shaking, Crazy Cold', 'crazy' collects much of what is outlandish, erratic, unpredictable, unreliable about old age: our muddles about time, our even greater muddles reading maps, especially following them upside down and then matching maps to the streets we're navigating, our failure to recognise places, faces, to remember names. Rochester's 'crazy' is not deranged, or not only that. It means falling to bits, being broken, impaired, mismatched, jagged, out of kilter. Yeats gets his 'Crazy Jane' to speak out, wild and inspired in her old age, and though I claim no kinship there, I recognise her craziness. Robert Burns uses the word tenderly to remind his old farmer's mare of what they have in common and what is still to come:

> Yet here to crazy age we're brought,
>   Wi' something yet.

While Robert Louis Stevenson doesn't include himself among

> The auld folk wi' the crazy banes,
> Baith ald an' puir,

seeing the old rather as figures in a vision or dream of the world's sufferings.

'This Life' is undoubtedly the property of the young, their moment, their acre, their sunlight. But here, wandering through it all, are the old, tottering, awkward, crazy, cackling and zigzagging their way towards the end, but also impudently here in what is after all our time and space too, no longer quite belonging to what we still possess and are possessed by, left stranded by our past, our supposedly best times, and averting our gaze so far as we can from the future.

2

On Not Wanting Things

My favourite sweater, brown and from Gap, is unravelling, on its last legs, in its death throes. I can't quite throw it away, or not until I'm sure it's absolutely beyond help, so I wear it to write in and to go swimming, usually with a dark, long-sleeved T-shirt under it to disguise or anyway mitigate the holes in its elbows. I'm wearing it now. It needs elbow replacements, as I've needed knee replacements. But if I were to go to the department in Peter Jones that sells leather patches to sew on its elbows I'd have to do something about the ragged sleeve ends that I roll up out of the way, and then these improvements would entail doing something about the neck and the bottom of the sweater, and so on and on. It needs, as I need, a clinic where all its drawbacks can be attended to at the same time, where someone could weigh the pros and cons of keeping it alive or letting it go: give an official verdict. Perhaps I would then be able to discard it or give myself over to its total renovation. Or even buy a new one.

This business of not wanting new things is beginning to unnerve me. I have lots of horrible old clothes with all too much wear left in them. They're relics from when I went to work every day, and I stopped doing that twelve years ago. So, though I'm nowhere near the position of King Lear's poor, bare, forked animal, I'm not quite far enough from being one of those old women whose clothes are fairly clean and tidy, but unimaginably out of date – several really serious sartorial decades out of date. I try to believe that my old flared jeans are back in fashion, that a granddaughter or two might be taken in. But they won't be. My flared jeans are subtly and disastrously different from anything they would consider wearing, and they're not quite 'Vintage' either. Yet ten years or so is nothing nowadays, after all. I have seen women like me wearing indestructible Horrocks dresses of the sort I coveted in the late 1940s, and even those little raspberry-coloured shoes with Louis heels from Dolcis, which were £3 19s 11d in the late 1950s. I actually owned a Horrocks dress or two in my teens. I remember that they cost what seemed an exorbitant £5 each. One of them was covered in huge sunflowers and had a circular skirt and a sailor collar. I expect that I moved heaven and earth to acquire those dresses. Yet I felt nothing but relief when a dress shop at the end of the road closed recently, presumably ruined by the recession. As purveyor of colourful shrouds for women exactly like me, I'd found it easy to resist. There is a woman I see quite often in the King's Road, on the other hand, almost certainly my contemporary, who has a straw boater perched on long blond hair, a red ribbon hanging

down her back and Courrèges boots with little squares cut
out of them. It's just possible that the long blond hair is fixed
to the boater and that they and the red ribbon come together
as a set. Muriel Spark had some white Courrèges boots in
the seventies, I remember, which she wore with a stiff little
dress like a sandwich-board made of playing cards.

Luckily, perhaps, my clothes were never very fashionable
in the first place, though now I come to think of it I had
some wonderful high brown boots made by Anello & Davide
that cost me £6 in the early sixties. I wore them to go to
New York to stay with my sister Rachel, when we were both
pregnant with babies who are now at least forty-five.
Jonathan, my sister's husband, introduced these two enormous sisters to people we met as Jane and Rachel Miller,
without explaining that we weren't both married to him and
bearing his children simultaneously. What happened to the
boots? They went with a long brown coat and a white sheep-
skin hat that made me imagine or hope that I looked a little
like Anna Karenina.

It goes against nature not to want new clothes: I used to
want them badly and all the time. I remember in the war
that once you'd spent almost the whole of a season's clothes
coupons on an item of school uniform you'd be lucky to
squeeze in a blue rayon dress with cap sleeves and a pair
of heavy brown walking shoes; and these with tap dancers'
metal segs affixed to toe and heel to stop you wearing them
out too fast. So I grew up dreaming of clothes and later made
some for myself from paper patterns: proper dresses with
belts and zips and darts and buttonholes, and once an elaborate

strapless evening dress with bones in it that I made for going to balls at university and never wore. I bought some beautiful black velvet jodhpurs in the sixties and a little later two skin-tight dresses with flared skirts designed by Mary Quant or Biba, that made you look as if you might be going skating.

My four granddaughters would rather shop than do anything else in the world, and one of them wondered especially idly the other day whether it might be possible to do a PhD in shopping, and of course it would. While I can hardly bring myself to go into a shop these days! If I do, I become instantly restless and despairing. There is nowhere to sit, nothing to want and absolutely nothing to buy. I congratulate myself when I actually manage to buy something, relieved that it is still possible, that I am able to part with money in exchange for something I didn't have before and don't need. When I get home with my new treasure I invariably discover that I already have several versions of the thing I've just bought: a black polo-necked sweater, Converse trainers, and so on. I have a page at the back of my diary for noting down things I've bought, and so far this year I've bought nothing for myself except two toothbrushes, some cough linctus and yesterday (what a triumph!) a suitcase on wheels. I went on an expedition the other day in my brown suede Converse trainers with yellow cut-out stars, in the hope of finding another pair just like them. But shoes like mine have long since gone out of fashion, and I came back empty-handed.

Of course some of this is simple parsimony, and I was brought up to that, both to practise it and to despise it, and to worry in all sorts of ways about money. I'm rather ashamed that I almost always remember the price of things. My father regarded parsimony as a virtue and prevented my mother from spending any of the money she inherited. In the end she became ultra 'careful' about money too, though her instincts were generous, I think. I have inherited both attitudes. I like giving money away, but I don't like giving people presents, because I'm always sure that my presents are exactly what they don't want. And I possess so many things I don't want that I hate to think of inflicting unwanted things on anyone else. But I like writing cheques for people, and in order to do this with the kind of flourish it needs I have to be sure I have enough money in the bank. None of this is selfless, by any means. I write about it now because I think these habits have hardened to grooves and hillocks in my nature and are now unalterable. Typically, cheques are frowned-on these days, and we're supposed to transfer money online. I have so far failed to accomplish this feat. The only time I tried I was so slow that the computer assumed I was cheating and refused to let me continue.

When I do manage to buy something, the pleasure I get from it is mainly in the thought that it will 'see me out', that this might be the last pair of socks, the last shirt, the last sweater I will ever need to buy. I am definitely on my last car. And far from feeling cast down by that thought I am restored by it to smugness and warmth, like some cosy, hibernating Beatrix Potter character, Mrs Tiggy-Winkle, perhaps, sensibly squirrelling away (if hedgehogs can be said to do that) for the winter ahead. The job's done, time has been saved, and I am braced for all weathers, floods, earthquakes and terrorist attacks.

Talking of which, I was visited recently by a friendly black policewoman, who wanted to know what I thought she and her colleagues should be doing about terrorists in Kensington and Chelsea. There have been a few in the north of the borough, and one of them left a bomb in a small weedy park where I'd walked with my grandson only the week before. The policewoman sat and dunked her biscuit and drank her tea while I tried to fill in the booklet she'd given me, which had pages of questions she wanted me to answer. Ideas fly off like starlings when I'm faced with multiple-choice questions. They never include the only question I'd have asked myself and might possibly be able to answer; and that scale from 'extremely' to 'not at all' never quite includes the level I'd have ordinarily gone for. And then there was – there always is – a space for other ideas, of which I have none, I'm sorry to say, about what should be done about terrorism. What could I say? I tried 'Arabic lessons for pensioners', 'more vigilance' and 'more bobbies on the beat', but she can't possibly have needed to hear that. What should the police be doing? How could I help them?

The policewoman was rather enjoying my warm kitchen and seemed not to mind me groaning and crossing things out. But I was suddenly sure that I really couldn't spend the rest of my life or even the next ten minutes waiting to be blown up by a suicide bomber and imagining what would have forestalled him, let alone discussing with neighbours and the police how this fate might best be avoided: for the policewoman had suggested that I join a local discussion group, which would recommend possible manoeuvres for the police to practise on the Fulham Road. I have once or twice been to protest meetings at my local town hall: most of them about plans to open a Christian Academy down the road, sponsored by the Diocese of London. Everyone at such meetings is very cross, though usually for completely different reasons: God, traffic jams, the fate of a particular eleven-year-old. A group planning to deflect a terrorist attack would be riven with dissent before it began its deliberations, though I suppose it might start by not excluding Muslim children from a spanking new school up the road.

Anyway, there's too much pretending to want our opinions these days. The BBC never stops asking viewers what they think about this and that, asking for trouble. What do they do with the replies they get? It's bound to inflame people, arranging to pool thoughts about terrorists; it might even excite a few terrorists and attract some who had hitherto shown relatively little interest in this part of London. All I could suggest in the end was that the police do less of all this, less stopping and searching and suspecting and upsetting people. Perhaps they should go back to tackling bullies and burglars and making the streets safe for children.

And there was I, worrying that I don't want things any more. I do seem to want to stay alive, though it's hard to imagine a long life stripped of all covetousness. I might stop wanting breakfast, for instance, or my bed, or company of any kind. There must be things I want, just as there were things Rupert Brooke loved. Perhaps I should list them as he listed his best things. Except that the things I want are not really on the cards. They're things like a swimming-pool under the basement of my house, some decent teeth and going to India every year on a magic carpet rather than in a Virgin aeroplane. And I don't really even want those things much. I feel about my house rather as I feel about my clothes. Apart from its own swimming-pool, it lacks for nothing that I can see. Yet most of the houses in the street where I live undergo nearly total renovation every other year or so. The changes are often so radical that the owners have to move out for months while the builders move in. As a result of my neighbours' most recent thoroughgoing transformations, I too have had several bits of my house painted, inside and out. I find myself doing little sums about how old I'll be before anyone is likely to point out that it needs painting again. It must have been nearly fifty years ago that Penelope Gilliatt, that clever writer, pointed out to me that she'd be thirty by the time the Hyde Park underpass was finished. I have thought of that every time I've driven through it. She meant that it would take ages – though she can only have been thinking of three or four years – that by the time the underpass was finished she would no longer be young, her life would have changed for ever. And I seem to remember that it had.

What I'm laboriously getting round to, I suppose, is the fact that the main thing I don't want any more is sex. This is a relief, but also a surprise. And I wonder whether desire for

things and people, covetousness, longings, are all aspects of
narcissism, or rather, whether they are all feelings related in
some way to pleasure in one's self. If I had known when I
was young that a time would come when I would get no
pleasure from inhabiting my body or looking at it, and no
excitement at the thought that it might be admired and even
desired by someone else, especially if delectably adorned –
or entirely unadorned – I suspect I would have thought it not
all that worthwhile continuing to be alive. Something like
that, no doubt, sends my delectable granddaughters on their
shopping sprees. It's true that when I had such feelings of
pleasure and sheer interest in myself they were spasmodic,
and often frail and challenged. They were, after all, precisely
the part of one's being most vulnerable to dips and depression, to losses of confidence. But they were there constantly,
if only as memory and hope. Without wanting things and
without feeling that there was something potentially attrac-
tive and, yes, desirable, about one's clearly otherwise
unremarkable self, it would have been hard to be in the
world, to enjoy it, to love and like other people, to long for
them, to face the future with avidity and energy. It can't be
a coincidence that one should be stripped of desire and of
being desirable and desired more or less in one fell swoop.
Rather a good arrangement, really. But if it makes for peace,
it also feels like an absence, a removal of one significant way
of being in the world, perhaps even a loss: though perhaps
not a loss of any greater significance than the loss of a front
tooth.

Presumably people do go on living quite comfortably

without narcissism, self-love, vanity? But without libido? Because I can no longer detect it in myself I suddenly realise what people mean by 'libido'. Not just desire, but a sort of greedy and even competitive energy. That's what I don't have any more. I always thought 'desire' an embarrassing word: I knew perfectly well what it meant, but I couldn't bring myself to use it. If it contained some kind of swooning, bliss-ful, heavenly sensation, it also had something barbaric and grasping about it, a fierce fury to have what one wanted in the teeth of opposition and of what other people wanted. *Désir* used to crop up a lot in Racine (somewhat improbably and changeably, I think now, after seeing *Andromaque* in French recently) and also in French feminist writing, I remember, where it seemed to be about rather more than sexual desire. It meant wanting in the sense of lacking, so it was about wanting what you lacked and didn't have (which was a polite way of saying that women wanted a penis, though it was more often referred to as a 'phallus' in the harder sort of feminist text, particularly the ones about Lacan, whose name so conveniently said it all). I was never sure that this really was what I lacked or what I wanted. Though I suppose it might have been thought to stand in for some of the particular kinds of wanting that women are all too likely to go in for. So is that what I no longer have? *Désir?* And has it just disappeared? Has the heart grown old?

Something very like desire is indeed missing now, alto-gether gone: so much so that I can hardly remember having such feelings, and I have to work hard to create some simulacrum of them in myself in order simply to pass muster as an adult female human being and avoid causing dismay to my nearest and dearest. But far from regretting the absence of such feelings, I am happier, easier, lighter without them. I was often buoyed up by sensations of longing and wanting. They gave potential excitement to my waking up, to a new day, a new week, a new year. But all that wanting was distracting, contradictory, laced with tripwires and danger. It entailed competition, fear of failure, risk, jealousy, embarrassment.

So there are real gains in being shorn of it. I was some-times so busy wanting things, people, love, praise, that I stopped looking at things, didn't notice trees and birds and buildings, as I do now. I forget people's faces these days and can't remember what they were wearing when I last saw them. Forgetfulness, no doubt, but also inattention, lack of interest. If there are gains in all this, and there are, it is also excluding and strange having to adjust to the disappearance of sex as a preoccupation when there is so much of it still going on in the world, visibly as well as invisibly. There are women of my age who have boldly, and usually shamefacedly, confessed to wanting sex now, preferably with a beautiful young man. I see the point of the beautiful young man, but none at all in the sexual act, though I'm greeted on most mornings by emails inviting me to enlarge my penis or pur-chase quantities of cheap Viagra, and my communicants, whose names change with each message, tell me they are nice girls, who just want to be my friend. Are they mis-reading my name or have I become the monstrously sexless old woman Dorothy Richardson so dreaded becoming:

'reverting later towards the male type . . . old women with deep voices and hair on their faces . . . leaving off where boys of eighteen began'?

Who sends us these messages about Viagra and penis enlargement? One of the messages has a small girl sitting next to a penis twice as large as she is and threaded with veins as if it were a painting on graph paper by Lucian Freud. What do these messages presume about me? In what category do I figure on their lists? I imagine a little office above a shop in Poland Street in Soho – with a dreadful lavatory on a half-landing, equipped with a patented cardboard mouse-trap – where a never-ending series of young recent graduates or, perhaps, teenagers on 'work experience', take their place at one of the two computers there and punch in the day's helpful message to some of the millions of names on their list of email addressees. Though it is more likely, given the times, that they are sitting in the penthouse of some glorious skyscraper. Poland Street belongs to my youth and the dispiriting job agencies I remember visiting when I'd just left university. Whichever it is, penthouse or Poland Street, you could see the presence there of those teenagers or shiny new graduates as the first step of a career in marketing. Could they imagine that for me those messages are simply a daily reminder of what I don't want any more?

I remember how warmed I could be just thinking and dreaming about sex, never mind wanting and having it. I also remember laughing at a friend of mine who seemed to regard sex as a bit like Ovaltine, good for sending you to sleep. And then I remember realising, probably quite late and in my twenties, what power it had over you and having to think all over again about everyone I knew in the light of that belated discovery. How troublesome we have all found its sheer force and insistence and how carefully we've disguised our interest and excitement. And how hopelessly it inclined one towards some people and not others, often regardless of their manifold charms or disadvantages. Now I am detached and curious, and I have rather solemnly to remind myself that various kinds of inexplicable human behaviour may well be provoked by untrammelled or over-trammelled sexual feeling of one kind or another. I read about love and attraction and people being in the grip of feelings they can't control, as in *Andromaque*, and I recognise what I read as you might recognise the general layout of a town you visited years ago or the rough storyline of a novel you read in your teens. Every now and again I read about very, very old people falling in love and looking forward to a rejuvenated sex life. I am astonished. I hear too that there are people as old as I am who go in for Internet dating, and that it's possible for them to find far more suitable mates online than they would if they left it to catching someone's eye at a party or on a bus.

Such thoughts may have helped to make reading Ian McEwan's *On Chesil Beach* especially interesting. It is a novel about a young married couple on their wedding night in the early sixties. McEwan's Florence and Edward are a little younger than I was then, but not much. It was a time when 'a conversation about sexual difficulties was plainly impossible', though, as McEwan quickly points out, 'it is never easy'. The period is important to the couple's predicament, however, as a time when such young people, more perhaps than at any time before or since, felt themselves 'bound by protocols never agreed or voiced', though these were not by and large protocols encouraging them to desist from sexual intercourse. Both of them are anxious about the night ahead, but whereas Edward's anxiety is healthily composed of worry about his own performance and excitement at finally achieving what has been rather puzzlingly denied him so far, 'Florence's anxieties were more serious'. She dreads what is to happen, but is too ashamed of her feelings, too determined not to hurt Edward's, and too guiltily aware that she should have come clean much earlier, to admit to her terrors. She is ignorant and inexperienced, and still hopes that what she feels may turn out to be unexceptional, alterable. She knows that the girls at her music college would have leapt into bed with their Edward months before marrying him and, equally, that there exist 'fabled girls' who are as keen on sex as Edward is.

Tenderly, carefully, without blame or explanation, McEwan describes the appalling hour or so in which Florence's fears of sex are realised and Edward's hopes entirely dashed. The marriage is over before it has begun. We're told a little of what happens to them afterwards. Florence, as first violin of her own quartet, does well as a musician. We know nothing, though, of her sexual life. Nor do we know whether her difficulties derive in some way from her mother's coldness and/or her own possibly incestuous relation to her father, which is imaginatively allowed for. Edward abandons his academic ambitions and becomes a rock music entrepreneur, has lots of affairs and a brief marriage before becoming stout and bald and oddly disconnected from the world, though not apparently unhappy. He recovers from what has seemed to him the humiliation of his wedding night and from the rage with which he reacted to it. Both Edward and Florence are affectionately understood, and though both of them come from what would nowadays be seen as differently dysfunctional families, McEwan fastidiously avoids explaining their sexual fiasco in terms of a family past.

The novel's power derives from this delicate balance between the particular predicament of these two people and its recognisable context. There have been other Florences in fiction, usually pathologised as frigid or potentially homosexual, but mostly shown to be tameable – and even finally tamed – by the right man. However, I can think of no other fictional young woman whose terror or horror of sex with a man is watched and understood in quite this way, nor embedded as hers is within its extraordinarily specific historical and social context.

Charlotte Brontë's eponymous Shirley and George Eliot's Gwendolen Harleth in *Daniel Deronda* are examples of young women who shy away from sex, though Shirley is finally 'managed', 'conquered' and 'governed' by the man she agrees to marry. Gwendolen is more like Florence, in her charm, her ambition and confidence, and in her spasmodic and debilitating terrors. Her reaction to her cousin Rex's love for her is, at first, evasion – 'having never had the slightest visitation of painful love herself' – and then, when he speaks out, revulsion, expressed by her words, 'Pray don't make love to me! I hate it.' Like Florence, she looks set 'to make a brilliant marriage', though that is by no means what she longs for. Nor, once she is married to Grandcourt, has she any thought of having children. George Eliot does not quite tell us about Gwendolen's married sex life with Grandcourt, though we are bound to infer that it is characterised by bullying and domination and that Gwendolen finds it unpleasant. Her terror is not named as sexual, though it is difficult to think of it in any other way, and as she gradually becomes more and more dependent on Deronda, it is clear that his androgynous appearance and personality are a major part of his appeal for her, a comfort, especially as he does not seem to be sexually drawn to her.

I experienced no such terrors as a young woman; but it seems – when I think about it now – that I was required to insert and contain my thoughts and feelings about sex within a curiously particular set of rules and regulations, which were never clearly articulated, were hard to make out, but also hard to resist. I remember feeling that my job was to reflect and even to act out a role created for me by the fantasies of strength and domination that any young man was bound to feel he ought to possess and exhibit; and that, by and large, my dreamy foreshadowings of what sex would be like were to be dismissed as thoroughly beside the point. There was, above all, a rash of D. H. Lawrence at the time. His novels were read by some of my male contemporaries as injunctions to have as much sex as possible. Nothing much was specified as to what this actually meant or why it was such a good thing, though as a friend of mine pointed out to me recently, Lawrence seems to be suggesting in *Lady Chatterley's Lover* that there's nothing like a daily dose of buggery for awakening and activating a woman's sexual desire. The question of possible conception was simply ignored (though I suppose buggery could be said to address this problem, if a little circuitously), perhaps because D. H. Lawrence himself was probably infertile.

This aspect of the times coexisted with other unclear, indeed unspoken, instructions. I knew that my parents had married because they thought my mother was pregnant. This, as it happened, turned out not to be the case, and I was born towards the end of their first year of marriage. Yet my mother quite often suggested that it would be better not to have sex until I was married, and both my father and my grandfather warned me at different moments about the intentions of the young men I was likely to meet at university – from, it seemed to me, some personal knowledge of what such young men were likely to be up to. Perhaps we all move into new kinds of anxiety when we become parents. Almost all the young women I knew in my college had affairs with men, sometimes serially, and in one or two cases with several at the same time, thereby occasioning farcical scenes, in which we all cheerfully collaborated, with young men whisked in and out of cupboards and boiler rooms in order to avoid detection or ugly scenes. The young women who didn't have lovers were thought likely to be lesbian or religious or strange in some way, or just resting. So we were liberated and thought of ourselves as liberated: a claim that seems to me both astonishing and mysterious when I consider it now. What did I think I knew that earlier generations had not known? And who had liberated me and from what? Even McEwan's Florence asked better questions and wondered more vividly in advance of it all than I did.

I am also amazed at how patiently we waited to be approached and chosen by men rather than approaching and choosing them, how meekly we undertook to guard, all on our own, against having babies, without any help from men, and how uneasily yet apparently willingly we – or perhaps I should say I at this point – consented to this inequality and imbalance in the interests of remaining trouble-free, popular and desired by men, who were in the vast majority at my university. We could easily have done a Lysistrata, denying ourselves en masse to these lusty Lawrentian undergraduates. You resisted or you succumbed, and when you succumbed you didn't discuss what you were doing with the person you were doing it with, nor did you talk much about it with your women friends. All this, I think, in the interests of what would now be thought of as 'cool', but also, of course, out of the most intense embarrassment, uncertainty, confusion, which I think of in hindsight as, collectively, the most powerfully determining array of feelings I experienced in those days. I have ever since thought of myself as hopelessly, but also shyly and uneasily, seduced by male desire and by the elaborate justifications that flourish in the world for its constant and free expression. So that over the years it has become difficult, if not impossible, to know whether fitting in with all that – as its object but also as its apparent champion – made it impossible to consider what I really wanted for myself. There was certainly a mismatch in my case between my apparent sophistication and my actual control or understanding of what I was getting into, physically, emotionally, even socially, and how this would affect my future life.

Not only do I think that in most respects my experience was very like that of my contemporaries, in this country anyway. I think that most young men and women are swept along by the narrative about sex that prevails among their contemporaries in the crucial years, their late teens and early twenties, and probably also by some form of resistance to what their parents have counselled on the subject or demonstrated in their own lives.

So I did not feel the terror that Florence and Gwendolen feel, but perhaps I should have done. I trusted to an alien rhetoric, I sometimes think, that was deaf to my experience and interests, and which could not accommodate my sexual feelings and needs or even allow me to consider them at all seriously. Accepting sex as above all natural, securely protected from the artificialities and contrivances of everyday life, was essential to all this, the sine qua non. From Lawrence we learned to skirt the dangers of 'sex in the head', so that the worst thing of all was to think or talk about sex. To protest would not only have been to argue with D. H. Lawrence, it would have been to defy nature. The deal, though, the reason why I and other young women put up with all this, was because we were flattered and excited by men's desire for us. I feel now that if I was taking foolish risks and putting myself outside any safe place where such matters could be helpfully and generously discussed, I had only myself to blame. And I was relatively chaste compared with some of my friends. But like Florence, I was exposed to the possibility of finding myself in a situation of extreme intimacy with the person least able to help me sort out my contradictory feelings about what was going on, precisely because of the way his feelings were implicated too.

It is this that McEwan understands so well: the impasse produced by kindly, affectionate feeling and the utterly different expectations of sex itself felt by an inexperienced young man and an inexperienced young woman. A couple like Edward and Florence are bringing their separate and different imaginative lives to a situation which simply can't bear their weight. I've almost never heard of anyone enjoying their first sexual encounter. Most of us, however, survive it, though perhaps less and less often with the person involved in that first, doomed episode. Perhaps I am being unfair to my young self just because I no longer recognise the emotions and the longings which guided me then, and because I am sometimes as much in the dark about that young woman in the late 1940s and early 1950s as I am about my granddaughters today and their burgeoning sixteen-year-old selves.

3

Dear Mary

Mary, my oldest, dearest friend, the repository of all my secrets, has Alzheimer's; or so they say. When a doctor first came up with this diagnosis, he asked her if she was the sort of person who wanted to know the truth about herself – to which, unsurprisingly, she had no answer – and then, if she knew what dementia was. 'Yes,' she replied, 'it means that you think I'm going mad.' The doctor seemed disappointed by this, as if he'd been poised to embark on a consoling tale about bits of us rotting with age: knees, feet, ears, eyes, teeth, and so on. And that with Mary it was her memory. Perhaps she was out to scupper his story.

My first sight of Mary more than fifty years ago was an elegant twirl on spindly heels. She was wearing a circular skirt of green felt with red patterns round its hem, bought in Florence, and I see it now against grass nearly as green as her skirt, somewhere inside Edinburgh University. My memory of her skirt overlaps with my memories of her paintings of late-summer landscapes that she'd brought back with her from Italy. We were both about to be married, and the men we were marrying had known each other for years and gone to the same school, though ten years apart. She told me later that she thought us very English and affected, with our 'darlings' and our rosy-cheeked sophistication, though Karl, whom I was marrying, was and thought of himself as Scottish through and through. Later, she and I were pregnant at the same time, though she gave birth first. And within two years she had had two babies, and the family had moved from Temple outside Edinburgh to London, where we were almost neighbours.

She told me about natural childbirth and how everyone in the class she went to fainted when they were first shown a film of a baby emerging bloodily but unassisted from its mother's womb. We walked both our babies in Mary's large pram along Kensington High Street, and they ate in a rather gingerly way the grapes we placed between them. And we talked and talked. Our two boys barely noticed one another in the pram as they eyed the grapes, though they were good friends later on. But then, after two years in London, the whole family moved to Strasbourg, and Mary had a third child before I'd had my second. It was while she was there and during her visits to England that our friendship bloomed. Sometimes her family came with her and were on their way to holidays in Scotland. Sometimes she came on her own to see an exhibition or to interview someone about Gwen John, the painter.

I think that as a child Mary, the middle one of three girls, always welcomed the prospect of growing up. She liked the adults in her life: her parents and all those aunts on both sides of the family, who had no children of their own and clearly delighted in their nieces. I imagine those three girls encircled by their mother and her sisters, and pleased to be; not at all likely to yearn for companions of their own age or to wish they were boys. Mary's mother could run like the wind and was the youngest of the sisters; the oldest was the 'posh' one, who lived in a big house with a gleaming husband: both of them, as I pictured them to myself, perpetually in evening dress, their hair stiffly lacquered as if for an Abdullah cigarette advertisement. Then there was the very small aunt, who gambled so successfully on the Stock Exchange and was thought to encourage burglars to call. Several aunts lived to be a hundred, as I expect Mary will. I have a feeling that one of them lost her wits at the very end.

So that while my stories of childhood were of awkward rebelliousness and uncertainties, of an absolute embargo on swank or congratulation, hers were full of assurance and success. She was the clever one, who prospered in the local high school. I learned from her that children can be successful children, good at being who they are; indeed, that we can all be successful at being who we are, or not. A friend once told me that the woman he was planning to marry was successful at wearing earrings. Mary might have thought that was going a bit far as a claim for the many forms success may reasonably take – or, perhaps, not far enough.

She learned to drive on her father's tractor at Gallamuir, near Stirling, in her high heels. I think of her thoughtfully working out the best way of covering the field with ploughed stripes before leaving for Edinburgh and an evening out. That must have been when she decided to study art there and was accepted for a course run jointly by the Art College and the University, so that her Double First at the end of it all encompassed four years of painting and four simultaneous years of Art History. And that was when she began her researches into Gwen John. I think I expressed amazement when I discovered that she had voted Tory at the last election. She was the only Tory I had ever had as a friend, or even known. I needed to explain this anomaly to myself, and I remember deciding that it was a product of the Scottish countryside, of her father and her family's farm where she grew up and of the stories she told me about her father taking two horses with him when he enlisted in the First World War as his contribution to the war effort. But she changed. Partly she was stung by the brutality of the Thatcher era. She discovered passionate moral feelings in herself, at once individualistic and egalitarian, which brought out the protester in her: against the poll tax and the elimination of post offices, for instance. She tried taking sides: the SDP for a bit and then the movement towards a Scottish parliament. But the obedience, the all or nothing, of party politics was not in the end for her, and she remained a maverick.

She was always impatient with attempts at consolation, with softenings of the truth, yet no one was ever better at soothing ruffled feathers and real pain. I told her things I've told no one else; though they were not things, I should say, of much general or dramatic interest. The point is that she loosened my tongue like no one else. I didn't just tell her things, I answered her questions about the things I told her. I wonder whether I did the same for her. Maybe I did, and I think of all those evenings Mary and I spent together – in Edinburgh, in a farmhouse in the Borders, in London and then in Bristol and once in the north-eastern corner of Spain – as a chain, several links of which had become narrow and wasted by time as well as distance, though it was never hard to return to the rhythmic divulging and receiving of stories or to the glasses of whisky and the countless cigarettes that were their accompaniment.

In the early days we waited for the children to be in bed and our husbands to be elsewhere. We talked about childhood and families as well as about our children and our husbands, about whom we sometimes made jokes. The occasional eccentricities of her husband, Robert, were referred to as 'robberies with violence'. And we talked about love and sex and work and painting and trying to do things like write and paint and teach when you were meant above all to be a devoted mother and wife. We talked about frustration and the small achievements and pleasures that occasionally found their way past it. We often disagreed. I was shocked that she stopped painting while her children were young. My mother had determinedly painted throughout our childhood. But Mary was always certain that she'd take it up again later, and she did. The whisky dwindled in the bottle and the toppling cairn of ash and cigarette stubs swelled and spilled, and there were times when we'd talk almost until morning and it was time for school and work. I discovered recently that one of my sons used to mark the point on the bottle where the whisky had started at the beginning of the evening.

It is impossible to imagine Mary apologising for the things that have happened to her or perhaps acknowledging a good many of them. She had no self-pity and no bent for self-disparagement. She was rare among people I've known for not complaining about old age or worrying, oddly enough, about losing her memory, or indeed about any of the other deleterious effects of old age. It was not her style. Nor did she change with age, though exasperation with the time-keeping of other people, particularly those involved with the railways and the speaking clock on the telephone, disguised for a time her increasing forgetfulness and then her gradual abandonment of any distinction between night and day. She digs her heels in now, and keeps her shoes on in bed when she feels like it, I believe. For a year or two I thought of all this as a particular kind of waywardness, produced by solitude. She had lived apart from her husband and happily alone for many years.

I sometimes wonder whether dementia is catching. It seems quite likely, I must say. John Bayley, in the book he wrote about Iris Murdoch, his wife, and her final years with Alzheimer's, recalls that it was difficult for him 'to remember a sequence of events; what happened when, in what order. The condition seems to get into the narrative, producing repetition and preoccupied query, miming its own state.' Whenever I've seen Mary in the last three years or so

I've tried afterwards to recall those details of her behaviour
that would have to be accounted odd or changed or wrong,
and I never can. They slip out of memory. I forget, rather as
she has forgotten, what seems inconsequential or non-
sequential and beside the point. The progress of her illness
is also hard to chart, though there are moments I remember
for my own bewilderment rather than hers. And the point
for me now is that she is there, but also not there, herself and
utterly without herself. Her idiosyncrasies have become a
way of entertaining us, and I think she feels it as a duty to
make us laugh. Dressing, washing, even eating, however,
have seemed especially beside the point to her, and she has
no interest at all in time. So there is no night for her and no
day, no mealtimes, no hurrying and no need to explain why
she's suddenly off and away.

Until recently, when she left her high and beautiful
Edinburgh flat where the *Edinburgh Review* was hatched in the
very first years of the nineteenth century, she used to take off
on her own, on long nocturnal jaunts. They were terrifying
for her family, though perhaps not for her. Now she walks
with what certainly looks like purpose along the corridors
of her new residential home, and up and down stairs, on her
strong, slim legs. She stops from time to time to gaze, rapt,
at a photograph or a postcard she's picked up and taken with
her, and reads aloud the words written on the back in what
seems a slightly mocking voice, though I can no longer guess
what the words might really mean to her. She tells us what
has just happened or is about to happen in that snap of herself as a child or in that carefully judged photograph of her

three children waiting for something or someone, bored stiff, by a pond full of model sailing-boats. The picture is given her full attention as she remarks on the way a leg crosses a patch of light, making a shadow that cuts the picture in two. It provokes one of her short, untethered narratives, which float free of any compulsion to satisfy her listener's silent 'So what?' as she gathers up possible moments from the past, only to slide disconcertingly off them, past them, creating as she goes little pockets of possibility outside the history those moments are still so full of. Some notion of time, it seems, survives, even if, as John Bayley puts it, 'time seems to lose both its prospective and its retrospective significance'.

No one could quarrel with the stories Mary weaves from the faint traces discoverable in an old photograph. Far from demurring or even feeling surprise at what she tells me, I find myself doggedly following her stories' shifts and lurches. It feels as if it's my fault if I find her hard to follow at times, even incoherent, and I am tense from the demands she makes on my attention, as I desperately hold out for some helpful and unravelling clue which will explain to me what's in her head. Her sentences are sentences, and her words are our words, after all. I share their associations, their public meanings, their scope for humour; and she is keen on puns and playing with words. She laughs and smiles a lot and I see none of that grim 'lion face' that Alzheimer sufferers are famous for. I think of memory as mostly reliant on imagination anyway, and of my own memories as too uncertain, too entangled in the language and the histories I've dressed them in, to stand in the least reprovingly against hers. And strangely, it is the inventions and dislocations of what she says that make me her mesmerised listener.

Those girls in their summer dresses and French sandals. Where are they now? Does she recognise them in the two loving women who visit her almost every day and take her out? And the boy? He is usually 'the boy' for her these days, though sometimes she gives him his father's name. Their photograph makes them entirely present to her as they were then. She knows something bad lies in store for the boy, but now at least she is safe from knowing quite what it is. What does she think of his elegant mother? Does she recognise herself? Does she have the difficulty I have in accepting that my young self and the self I now inhabit are in some pretty abstract way the same person? How could you possibly know that if you've forgotten how time works? Does she think of the Mary in the photograph as full of secrets, ones she still knows as well as ones she's forgotten? And does she realise that she has possession of my secrets too? What can she have done with them all? Have they flown like those birds she used tenderly to watch on her windowsill as they took off from the Meadows in Edinburgh for some Arctic waste, or has she tucked them into a private compartment of herself and thrown away the key? I feel my questions flying off with the secrets and the birds. The truth is that they are addressed to Mary, and only she could possibly answer them. Yet they mean a good deal less to her than that dying moth on her windowsill.

If I write to you, Mary, which one of you reads what I

write? The new one who knows who I am, but only just, or the old one, who wished me well and cheered me on, who remembered my stories better than I did, who could remind me of what I'd thought or said ages before and where she had had to disagree. I think of that special Scottish 'Whissht' you used to emit, dismissing nonsense with a whistle of good-tempered exasperation. Even quite recently, you managed a 'Good for you!' when I told you I had a book coming out. Everything I've written has had you in it somewhere, and this one did too. You were my constant interlocutor. You're there in my book reading that letter Gwen John wrote to my great-uncle, Michel Salaman, in 1933 about my parents bringing me up in Paris, 'all on their own', as she wonderingly put it. That phantom meeting, when you read that letter months before you and I actually met, gleamed through more than fifty years of friendship. It was a meeting between you as a serious young woman embarking on your research and the unknown offspring of what must have seemed to you and to Gwen John a pair of feckless bohemians, who probably forgot all about that small middle-aged woman peering into the pram and writing home about it in the letter you found. Everything else began from there.

Remembering was one of Mary's talents, as it happens. Remembering and analysis. She remembered the smallest details of our conversations, exactly what I'd said and what she'd said. What we were both wearing when Tony White died and we went to Kew on that cold, cold January day and sat huddled together on a wooden seat, crying and laughing and remembering what we'd thought and said to each other

five years before that, when Alan had died and we'd watched
the sun go down behind the Cheviots, which were spread
out before us like a patchwork quilt. That day, it had been
warm and well into May. She always remembered the
weather and what we were wearing, as well as what we'd
said, our actual words. She still has the words. They're as
clear and exact as ever, but emptied now of all those times
and sights and feelings. The words lead her somewhere else.

Amos Oz remembers wanting to be a book when he grew
up. Mary has become the strings of words, the sentences she
utters, their internal grammar as firm and intact as her body
and its sturdy skeleton. It is the relation of her words to the
world that is fractured, dislodged; though the real problem
lies somewhere else. Her speech no longer participates in
conversations. And though she seems to want to entertain
us, I'm not sure that she knows or cares whether we follow
her thoughts, agree with her words. Ordinarily, we would
have steered our way through our conversations, as people
do, checking for possible misunderstandings, differences:
deploying those crucial linguistic devices that children learn
almost as they learn to speak – tag questions, requests for
confirmation, resentful reminders: 'But you said . . .'
Without such doubts and queries and without their expression, language seems to float off, slipping the mind's noose.
Besides, Mary's 'now', and so mine too, is forever alluding
to a 'then' she's lost interest in. I want to stop her in her
tracks and suggest we go over it all again together, slowly
calling up memories and memories of memories, circling
them, casually nudging each other with little allusions and

reminders. I love all that reported speech, that amending and correcting of memories, that negotiation of truths. I would cheerfully waive my usual distrust of the pluperfect, especially when it's used for the cheaty fill-in flashbacks of novels, to hear Mary recall a moment we lived through together. It's not just that she's lost interest in the past. It sits there still as the material her mind works with. But it's infinitely malleable now, remakeable, unfixed. People crop up in her stories from before they were born and in places where they've never been. As in dreams.

The fact is that she much prefers the past she invents for herself, with help from pictures, words, names, objects. Her invented past is as populated as our shared one ever was and is of great – if transitory – interest to her. The same names and places turn up in it, but her versions of the past may now be miraculously emptied of trouble and pain, of deaths and betrayals and shame. The lines are down between us. If we still use the same words, they've lost their old meanings, the ones rooted in particular conversations and conversations about conversations. Without conversations, the past we shared has become a muddied pool, full of things I can't make out any more, movements under the water that I sense but can't follow without her, because it was always she who started the remembering and could be relied upon for that. I've read a little about autism and am surprised that its features are not more often likened to the effect of Alzheimer's on people, for in both, an entire system of empathy and imagination is impaired.

Mary preferred to live in the present even then. She felt

at home there and knew how to give herself to what she was doing, recognising potential pleasure as well as purpose in activities I thought dull, like washing nappies or preparing children's meals. She never rushed such things or skimped them, as I did. Where I was intent on freeing up portions of time in order that they be stripped of duties and available in principle for a multitude of far better things – like talking to Mary – and where I was also a believer in the dictum that a thing worth doing is worth doing badly, she hated to think of a single moment of her life being sacrificed or even subordinate to any other moment. It was a kind of democracy of experience. She disapproved of heavy distinctions, but also of any careless optimism about better times ahead. Too risky, too profligate. Each moment deserved proper respect. Sometimes I thought of this as an excuse for curbing her own ambition, both as a painter and as a writer. Her standards were too high for her own good, I used to tell her, her eye and her ear too fastidious. When she was writing about Gwen John, the subject of a lifetime's detailed and vivid research, and perhaps an alter ego, she was slowed down, sometimes to a standstill, by her determination to get it right, to say precisely what she thought the truth to be. Occasionally I managed to persuade her to dictate to me what she wanted to write, to let me take it down like a stenographer, so that at least she had a text to object to, to edit and rewrite. Perhaps I could have pushed her beyond the barriers she set up for herself, so that she'd have completed the biography she had started on, done so much work for. The short book she produced was beautiful, though not quite the biography she'd planned. She was wonderfully sympathetic to Gwen John, and quite without either the heavy reverence or the conventionality of John's other biographers. But I never dared to bully Mary, and I sometimes felt her fastidiousness as a rebuke: that I was too easily satisfied compared with her. These differences were vital to our friendship. We took very little for granted about each other and we were propelled by all that we had to explain to one another about ourselves.

And now, not quite a fly in amber, she is permanently fixed in the present. She does a quick dance routine with a napkin on her head, half Highland fling, half ballet lesson, and I remember that even-handed view of time, that clarity, that assurance about what mattered and what didn't. Talking, scrutinising photographs and postcards, singing, dancing, making jokes, telling stories: these things are her life now. I sense or perhaps want to read into her antics a mutinous insistence still that those things are worth as much as painting a picture or writing a book. And, as it happens, those are the moments I remember when I'm not with her, when I'm struggling to imagine her life now and what it must be like, stranded as she is for ever out of my time and inside her own.

There were her odd shoes, for instance, though there is less of that sort of thing now that her carers look after her morning routine. While she was still living alone in her flat, she sometimes told you, as that day's visitor, about her clothes and shoes. She showed me the neat – unnecessarily neat, as she saw it – piles of clean clothes 'they' had laid out for her on the bed where I used to sleep when I stayed there. She could see no point at all in them. If tomorrow is unimaginable, tomorrow's clean clothes are also unimaginable. Repetition is the condition of her life but also an irritant. Why do the same things have to happen every day? What was wrong with yesterday's version?

The moment I arrived on one visit, I remember, she showed me the best way of dealing with the long tail of her shirt by flinging her skirt over her face and showing how satisfactorily her shirt hung down beneath it. It felt like a problem solved once and for all. Then she sat down to gaze at her feet stretched out before her, as if she were in a shoe shop. She had a shoe on one foot, a boot on the other: 'I like this one very much,' she remarked of the shoe in a self-congratulatory tone of voice. 'And this one is useful,' she mused of the boot. Since she has been in the residential home near the iron-grey waters of the Forth, her shoes match and her hair is tied back in a ponytail. She took off one of her pretty pumps the other day, the ones they'd chosen for our visit, and recited the name of the shop – Russell & Bromley, written on the inside sole – where she must have bought them long ago. First she said the words in a posh London voice, mine perhaps, and then she sang them in reverse order. She often does accents: broad Scots and Morningside, then French – colloquial one minute, with a deplorable 'English' accent the next. It feels as if she's teasing, laughing, even censuring us for our earnestness and monolingualism. The last time I saw her she led us on a tour of the home, inviting us to peep into other people's rooms, the common rooms, the dining room where she refuses to eat, the stairs. She read the menu for yesterday's supper pinned to the wall. No one, she said, had enjoyed the tinned peaches and cream. She twirls and dances for us again, puts things on her head. When we left to go home, she must have thought for a moment she would be coming with us, and I can't forget her outstretched arm and her fingers delicately touching the closing glass door with its computerised lock. But perhaps I will forget, just as she has. She didn't look sad. Sometimes I think she may never have been happier.

Something has happened that has transformed her, and I don't begin to understand what it is. So I am bound to think of her still as accepting this extraordinary event with the same sangfroid with which she met all those other changes in her life, and most of all, Alan's death, though nothing was quite the same for any of us after that terrible day nearly forty years ago. We had an old American friend to dinner that evening, and when I explained to him what Mary had just told me on the telephone, I remember bungling the telling, nervously chattering about the recent exploits of our two sons, Mary's and mine, Alan and Daniel, fourteen years old both of them, who had been climbing Arthur's Seat a week before and seemed too often to court danger. Our friend took from what I told him that Alan was somehow more than reckless, that he must have meant to fall down that cliff near North Berwick, or that in climbing halfway down the cliff to retrieve his sweater he had enjoyed the risk of falling, done it with his eyes open, as it were, and that one should be philosophical about such things if they were the result of what people wanted, even if the people were still children. I felt it as culpable and characteristic of me, as it would never have been of Mary, that my account of what had happened should have misled my hearer, come out wrongly. Because there was never anything in the least self-destructive about that fall. It was an accident, and Mary, who watched it happen, never thought of it as anything but an accident. She already knew that he was going to die when she rang us, and she knew that during the next day or the one after that she would have to give permission to switch off his life-support machine. She had been sitting all day in the hospital drawing him with the bandage round his head, when she rang. And I think it was the following day that she told us, calmly and with no tears, that he'd died. We went to Edinburgh at once and stayed there for the funeral. I remember getting a harsh letter from my headmaster telling me that my pay would be docked because the funeral was not, after all, for 'a close relative'.

I look for continuities and am comforted when I find them. I want to read the old determination to resist dependence or foolish expectations into Mary as she is now, a person who must be perpetually, tactfully, looked after. What is so hard to make sense of in this strange illness is that it entails the utter disruption of all that we've come to know and expect of a person and the emergence of something familiar and normal at the same time. It is as if this new version has lain dormant during all those years, waiting to assert itself. Its appearance is simultaneously shocking and soothing, for even its most outlandish manifestations seem intimately part of the person who has been translated from one state into another but must somehow always have had it in her to change in just this way: so that her present self appears to have emerged from the shadows of her earlier life and quietly, without fuss or argument, taken its place.

And now there are no more stories. A fit during this last autumn put paid to them and to her happy wanderings. Now she sits, immobile, eighty or more, in her old rocking-chair, though it no longer rocks. She cannot move her hands or her feet or voluntarily open her mouth to eat or drink. She stares at my face and the faces of her other visitors with a look of steady intelligence, yet I am not sure that she knows any of us or even whether she knows anything at all. She laughed once in response to her daughter's laughter. Strange little phrases trip out, each repeated fast and several times: 'She would have been', 'Yes, I thought so too', 'It may be, yes, perhaps it is.' These are strangely complex bits of language, relics of a conversational life that is over, but which something in her remembers and wants to perform. Is vestigial anxiety and a need to hold anxiety at bay all she is left with now, with her reiterated 'Oh dear, oh dear, oh dear', 'All right, all right, all right' and 'Very good, very good, very good'?

4

Reading into Old Age

I couldn't be doing with John Updike's novel *Couples* when it came out in 1968. Too near the knuckle, I suppose, that novel about middle-class men and women in their thirties and forties making a mess of their marriages. And all told from a man's point of view, and a man who was almost exactly the same age as I was. I don't think I even managed to finish it, and that's unusual for me. I returned to Updike in old age, though, and now I wonder whether he regretted killing off his late-twentieth-century *homme moyen sensuel* at the end of the fourth of his *Rabbit* novels. Rabbit would only have been in his middle sixties at the beginning of any volume 5 if it had come out in the year 2000 and followed the pattern Updike established of a decade between each book; but we leave him finally when he is still in his fifties, his death caused by snacking and exasperation with his family rather than ennui. Would writing about, let alone living through, his sixties, his seventies, perhaps his eighties, have been so unbearable? And would reading about those years be unbearable too? Simone de Beauvoir thought so.

If an old man is approached subjectively he will not be a good hero for a novel; he is at the end of things, fixed, with no expectation of hope or development. The die is cast for him and he is already inhabited by death, so that nothing that may happen to him is of any importance. Moreover, a novelist can identify with a man younger than he is, because he has already been that age himself, but he only knows old people from the outside. So he gives them only minor parts, as a rule, and his portraits of the old are frequently sketchy or conventional.

There are a few writers who have ignored her warnings, though not many. Saul Bellow wrote *Ravelstein* when he was in his eighties. It is a novel about death and dying in which an old man – who is both its author and its narrator – keeps his promise to write the memoir of his younger friend Ravelstein, who is dying of Aids. Ravelstein's extravagant personality and life are filtered through his months of dying. He is a gay academic who, late in life, has become rich and famous as the author of a vastly popular book presenting his contentious and not entirely graspable ideas. Bellow, in his twin roles, lives through and learns from his friend's dying, which is stoically and often humorously borne. There are moments when the two men seem to be rivals in a race towards death, so that Ravelstein's getting there first propels his friend into a desperate illness, which nearly kills him, and which erupts in sympathetic and competitive mimicry. Bellow has his narrator believe, or half believe, that he will meet Ravelstein and members of his own family soon in some sort of heaven. In his last years, as Bellow put it to Martin Amis in an interview, 'I've reckoned with death for so long that I look at the world with the eyes of someone who's died.' One scene in the novel has a healthy middle-aged couple, who have been trying out a Thoreau-like existence in the woods, consult the dying Ravelstein about their proposed suicide pact. Ravelstein patiently hears them out before advising them to leave the woods at once. 'Nature and solitude are poison,' he tells them.

Bellow died at ninety, and this novel that he wrote in the middle of his last decade presents old age as a time filled with other people's deaths. It's certainly true that we approach our own death through a series of rehearsals or dummy runs. We go to a lot of funerals. Some of us wonder about our own funerals and whether anyone will come. We watch our parents do it and then our friends, and we match ourselves against them. We deliver elegies and write letters of condolence and, we hope, of consolation. We offer our help and our affection, and though neither may be taken up, we involve ourselves in the rituals and sadness of other people's death, almost as a prophylactic. So that our terror of death may be a little mitigated by familiarity and repetition. Ravelstein admonishes his friend, 'There are significant facts that have to be lived with but you don't have to let them engross you.' It is an admonition Bellow considers but ignores. He *is* engrossed, and so are we, in the imaginative procedures involved in responding to and getting ready for death.

Simone de Beauvoir is surely wrong to suppose that old age and its preoccupations lie outside the scope of novels, that the thoughts of the old and dying are bound to be static and uninteresting. Change is intrinsic to growing old and to the drama of dying. Indeed, the speeding-up of time in old age could be said to invite the unities and abbreviations – and the climactic prospects – of drama. On the other hand, de Beauvoir was entirely right to remind us that we have almost never heard about these moments and events from old people who are also poor; and many of the old are, and always have been, poor. Yet one explanation for the apparent silence of the old and poor is that large numbers of them are less likely to survive to a great age, and if they do survive they are less likely to write about their experiences. So you could say that there is a kind of luxury and privilege attached to such meditations as do exist, some self-indulgence.

There have been studies of old age, sociological, historical and medical, and of government policy and provision for the old; and telling figures have continued to emerge that spell out the scandalous differences that still exist between the old-age experiences of the rich and those of the poor. Wealth and class still have a significant impact on the mental and physical health of the old and on their attitudes to retirement and what goes on during those years. They also crucially affect survival rates and general longevity.

In the 1950s Peter Townsend, as his contribution to the Institute of Community Studies investigations into the structures of family life in Bethnal Green, concentrated on old people living in the East End. He wrote *The Family Life of Old People* and later another book about the homes and other institutions in England and Wales where many old people ended their lives, as they still do. It was always an important aspect of this school of sociology that their investigations would deliver far more than statistics. Both of Townsend's books are unusual for the detail and the variety of his evidence and for his unwillingness to generalise. Even in the mid-1950s there were people who lamented the destruction of family support systems in working-class communities, though Townsend's work made it clear that many of these were, in fact, still functioning in London's East End. He also showed that though his informants shared a geography and, up to a point, a culture, they were as different from one another as any other group of old people. The men and women he interviewed might live in complete isolation, or with a spouse, or with a whole range of family members in the same house or flat, or nearby. Yet there is also a woman, for instance, who bumped into a brother in the street, near where they both lived, whom she hadn't seen for two years. Townsend includes much of what people actually said in answer to his questions, and he also includes selections from four of the twelve diaries he asked some of his old men and women to write about their daily lives.

From all this, they appear to be a remarkably unself-pitying group of people, who expected to look after themselves and each other. They had very little money, and there were not many excitements in their lives, nor much variety. Almost all of them began the day with the lighting of fires and the feeding of pets: birds, dogs, cats. Shopping was daily and local, usually just enough for the day. I didn't have a fridge in those days, and clearly most of these people didn't either. None of them had a phone, and when they called the doctor they used a public phone box. One or two watched television occasionally in the home of a son or daughter. Most of them bought a newspaper every day, usually the *Mirror* or the *Express*, and sometimes, especially on days when the newspapers went on strike, one or two turned to reading books. Those with no immediate family seemed on the whole to have friends or acquaintances nearby and some of them went to the pub to play cards and to see friends. Perhaps the most enviable aspect of their often hard and lonely lives was frequent visits from children and grandchildren who lived nearby, though this was true only for a few. But the relation between grandparents and grandchildren seemed genuinely close and important to both sides. Old women were, on the whole, closer to their daughters than to their sons, but so were the men. The expectation was that daughters would look after you, and that daughters-in-law might present a problem for some, probably because they were busy keeping in touch with their own families, though this isn't actually voiced. I felt warmly for the seventy-three-year-old man who wrote in his diary, 'Had a long chat with the son about different things in life.'

*

Updike's Rabbit dies of a second heart attack in a Florida given over to the aged and wealthy and their intolerable boredom, though during the week or two before he dies he discovers another world behind the coastal condominiums there, of poor black youngsters as in love with basketball as he'd been in his youth. But he is already too old and exhausted, we are made to feel, to do more than dip a toe into other, unknown worlds like this one, however enticing they may be – and this one is actually pretty rebarbative, in spite of its seductions. The gap between the inhabitants of condominiums and the young men who might, if they're lucky, get jobs as servants in them is too wide to bridge.

Rabbit starts to read history at the end of his life, and though he can't always concentrate 'he finds that facts, not fantasies, are what he wants' in his reading and on television. But the discoveries he makes tell him only that it is too late for him to remake his life in the light of new knowledge and experience, or, as he puts it in his own head, in not quite (you feel) his own words, it is too late 'to be serious, to reach down into the earth's iron core and fetch up a real life for himself'. Many of us have been possessed at times by thoughts that the life we are living is not the real one, but some botched job we somehow fell into, provisionally as it were, fine for the time being, until we've decided what we really want to be or do. Old age certainly sorts that out for us, and may come to seem an improvement on a lifetime of provincial try-outs. Saying to yourself that this is it, all it was ever going to be, has its consolations. Rabbit, you might say, dies after a series of dress rehearsals in mid-first night: 'a happy release' according to some, 'a good way to go', but an abrupt foreshortening for others.

Carolyn Heilbrun, the feminist thriller writer and academic, promised herself and the world that she would commit suicide at seventy, but when she got there and began to reflect on the past ten years, her dreaded sixties, she realised that she had enjoyed them, had changed, learned things, broken out, and she proceeded to write a book about those years called *The Last Gift of Time*, in which she considered why those years had been so much better than she had expected. She relished her escape from the poisonous, pompous malice of the academy and what she felt as its contempt for women; she forgot about skirts and high-heeled shoes, she learned to take pleasure in her husband and children, to get her own way (it's a bit hard to believe that this was for the first time) and to be guarded about the past and about memories. So she deferred her suicide for seven years, until 2003; and it isn't possible to say whether this suicide resembled as an undertaking the one she had always planned, in order, as she put it, to quit while she was ahead. She certainly double-checked, with a plastic bag as well as pills, I believe.

Her friendship with the older May Sarton, who lived into her eighties, is one of the pleasures of those years that Heilbrun recalls in her final book. She remembers the older writer's rages at the 'respected critics' who neglected her work, and even at Heilbrun herself. But it was not her rages, and not the critics, that defeated her, but her own body, and Heilbrun learned the lesson. Rages, Heilbrun seemed to

feel, kept you alive and well. Rabbit is brought down by his
body too, by its smothered and ever diminishing traces of a
strong, athletic youth and by his ruinously tender indulgence
of it. Carolyn Heilbrun refused to wait for even the first
signs of morbid deliquescence. Rabbit hopes 'he never
reaches the point where he has to think all the time about
shitting'. We all hope that. Both of them got out early.

There are people who proudly deny that their age makes
the difference. What is wrong is wrong with the world and
not with them. The comedy of ageing is the only aspect of
the subject that gets relatively short shrift in de Beauvoir's
impressively synoptic *Old Age*. The comedy often emerges
from those moments when a newly awakened sense of the
absurd fads and fashions of other people combines with a
glimmering perception that perhaps we are not moving with
the times and that these discrepancies and incongruities so
striking to us may actually be invisible, and certainly insignif-
icant, to people younger than ourselves. The poet Hugo
Williams, who is not yet seriously old, ends an essay on the
subject with Petrarch's grim assurance that old age changes
us to the point where we are unrecognisable, even to ourselves. 'I shall not seem myself: another brow, other habits,
a new form of mind, another voice sounding.' But Williams
is funny precisely because he doesn't quite believe that. He
is changing, but it is he who recognises that his impatience
with mobile phones and his pernickety objections to other
people's use of English are the beginning of his own end rather
than the world's.

None of us wants to believe that, of course. Nor do we

want to accept the myriad ways in which we have been slowly and imperceptibly turning into our parents, nor that suddenly the process has speeded up. That old pair we out-stripped so effortlessly, casually putting them right about the modern world, defending our generation's linguistic slippages and inventions, as well as the Rolling Stones and mini-skirts, against their scepticism, their better taste and loftier standards: suddenly we're them and they're us. Now it is I who mock with hollow, unappreciated scorn the goose-pimpled bare bellies, the jeans slung so low on the hips by their young male wearers that a week's rations might be stored in their pendulous seats, the dangerously skyscraper shoes, the ruinous tattoos that will be so bitterly regretted, the studs in lips and nostrils. And I am mocked in my turn, reminded by my youngest granddaughter that it is I who am hopelessly out of kilter, not the young. These are, after all, the fashion. Don't I know about that?

It is a strange moment; one that may begin to happen before our parents die, though its meanings visit us more savagely afterwards, and it is a blow to more than our vanity, besides having a funny side, as Hugo Williams shows:

I do exhibit certain symptoms – fear of the young, indus-triousness, nostalgia, the realization that I am less cool than I have previously thought, and the conviction that changes in society are a personal insult. I impersonate my father as an amusing ploy, then become angry when I am taken seriously. How he effected the miraculous trans-formation from male lead to heavy father is the technique that is currently being revealed to me. I'm learning fast. Already I have mastered the twitches of irritation around the mouth, eyes screwed in pain as I examine the ridiculous over-abundance of choice on the sauce shelves at Sainsbury's.

One certainty of age is that everything has got 'worse', but this may possibly be an illusion. When having your hair cut, you gradually give in and stop protecting the top of your head as if it were an area of great natural beauty. You don't want to put hairdressers off by saying, 'Leave it long on top', but if you say nothing they attack it as if it were no different from the sides and back, and pretty soon you have a short-on-top haircut like everyone else.

Julian Barnes brought out a collection of stories called *The Lemon Table* in 2004. They are all about old people and growing old, and one of them invents the letters a clever, scholarly old woman writes to a relatively young novelist, whose *Flaubert's Parrot* she has heard of, though not yet read. She has always preferred 'serious works' to fiction, and faced now with the romances provided by the Red Cross trolley, she can only ridicule their clichés; and, as she tells him, 'even at an age when I might have been susceptible to such an implausible view of life, I preferred Darwin's "Vegetable Mould and Earthworms"'.

But she does begin to work her alphabetical way through the novels in the library, and she's got to B. Her letter-writing friendship with the more or less fictional Barnes is told only through her very funny letters, as she stores his in the refrigerator and they rot when the power is turned off after her death. Her letters manage to suggest a whole life seen from and lit by old age, and this is rare. Hers are never dim, sepia memories, winnowed out of nostalgia. They are framed by age and by the rememberer's current and brilliantly seen life in an old people's home, where she has installed herself at eighty-one, and where she dies three years later. It is hard to believe that her letters are not based on those of a real-life person, so wonderfully particular is she as a character, so exactly are her idiosyncrasies and even her speech caught by how she writes: 'The only book of yours you told me not to read was the only one available at the library. "Before She Met Me" has been taken out 11 times since January, you will be fascinated to know, and one reader has heavily scored through the word "fuck" whenever it occurs.' Only in her two short last letters is there the least hint of confusion, and that confusion crackles compared with the two ill-written missives that follow, thudding through the Barnes letter-box and announcing in the formal, treacly language of her professional carers that his old pen-friend has died.

Perhaps it is a particular kind of energy that I am looking for in accounts of old age, an energy released and realised by all those curtailments on adventure and ambition and the need to please. John Updike may have funked it with Rabbit, but he delivers something like it in his more recent novel about a seventy-nine-year-old woman called Hope, who is a painter and a widow of painters (she is based on or has been likened to Lee Krasner, who was married to Jackson Pollock). Updike's novel, called *Seek My Face*, consists of a day-long interview with Hope, conducted by a serious young woman from New York, about the painter's life and work. The details of these emerge, predictably snagged by detours into the lives and work of Hope's three husbands, so that the day and the novel become a matter of retrieving the past and of the effect this has on the two women's interest in one another. This moves from chilly, suspicious circlings towards some affection and sympathy. But also, telling her story, remembering it for this young woman, creates in Hope what she thinks of as a 'sense of compressed simultaneity', for the day's interview has left her with 'the disquieting sensation that the events of her life have been too close together, compressed into a single colorful slice of time rather than unfolding in an organic sacred slow process of nights alternating with days, phases of solitude and uncertainty and desolation'.

The novel is concerned with the material of memory, its contents, but also with its distortions and reductions, its formal arrangement of the fragments it has to make do with, its subservience to the needs of the present. It is not only that one's memories don't match the original, nor even that they either wilfully or unintentionally falsify the truth. It is that being old makes being young look quite different. Hope often sits in judgement on her past self and on the characters of her youth, just as she sits in judgement on her young female interrogator; but working to answer her questions, satisfy her curiosity, also makes it possible for Hope to forgive her own youth, to like her young self better. And those false, overworked sequences and moments that memory has retrieved from the past are transformed to become her paintings, which are, as it happens, abstract and almost monochrome — like black and white photographs and most of our dreams — just as they become the material of Updike's novel.

It may be chance that it is old women rather than old men that Barnes and Updike write so well about. In an earlier book, *Writing a Woman's Life*, Carolyn Heilbrun claimed that women only learn to express their anger once they are past fifty, and she linked this to the differences she perceived in the way women and men experience old age: 'It is perhaps only in old age, certainly past fifty, that women can stop being female impersonators, can grasp the opportunity to reverse their most cherished principles of "femininity".'

Simone de Beauvoir thought that growing old was easier for women than for men. She thought that they had less to lose in the way of work, status, power and that they retained their role and function in families and communities, at least in some cases. There was even the possibility of a kind of liberation for them, a rest from serving other people. They could begin to concentrate on themselves.

There is, in addition, a somewhat unreliable but popular myth that old age will release women from a lifetime of being good girls, of striving to win points for virtue. Frances Cornford put it as a question 'To a Fat Lady seen from the Train':

Why do you walk through the fields in gloves,
Missing so much and so much?

*

She was answered by a stampede of women promising to behave as badly as they could in their old age, to live out a joyful second childhood. The two tipsy old ladies causing sweet mayhem in the aeroplane at the end of Margaret Atwood's novel *Cat's Eye* console her heroine for the brutal rivalries that have always marked her friendships, first with girls and now with women:

> They seem to me amazingly carefree. They have saved up for this trip and they are damn well going to enjoy it, despite the arthritis of one, the swollen legs of the other. They're rambunctious, they're full of beans; they're tough as thirteen, they're innocent and dirty, they don't give a hoot. Responsibilities have fallen away from them, obligations, old hates and grievances; now for a short while they can play again like children, but this time without the pain.

Jenny Joseph's 'Warning' won a popularity poll for poems in Britain, presumably for its charming, perhaps too charming, account of how she planned to conduct herself as an old woman, reverting to childhood, learning to spit, sitting down on the pavement whenever she's tired and feels like it. Clearly the poem touched a nerve, even if sitting down on the pavement would be an impossibility for most of us. These are somewhat sweetened versions of the disagreeable old witch of fairy stories. Atwood's old girls and Jenny Joseph's old tearaway must somehow strive to keep their looks, stay girlish and continue to insist that 'You've got to laugh.'

If John Updike doesn't quite bring Rabbit back to life or force him to endure old age like the rest of us, he did write a short millennial sequel to his *Rabbit* novels, in which Rabbit is remembered ten years after his death by his son and his wife and his hated old friend, who is now married to Rabbit's wife. A long-lost daughter turns up and wants to know about this father she'd barely met. She learns that he was 'beautiful' and 'childish', epithets which Rabbit would not have used about himself. Time and this new sister have tempered the son's grudging memories of his father, and he has come to believe at last that 'Dad didn't want to wait around and become an old guy. He didn't have the patience' – or, perhaps, the nerve.

Tolstoy's Ivan Ilyich dies before he is old, in what should have been the prime of life, from a mysterious illness caused by an injury acquired during a spell of what would be thought of nowadays as innocent home improvement or DIY. Tolstoy himself was nearly sixty when he wrote *The Death of Ivan Ilyich* and had another twenty-four years to live, but in its mercilessness the story already bears the marks of his conversion to the thunderous moralism and hatred, especially of his wife (and, I suppose, of himself), which characterised the many later years of his long life. He hates Ivan Ilyich for his ordinariness, though he has been a successful judge, and even for the smug and unimaginative pleasure he derives from decorating his apartment according to the fashions of the day. The hatred thunders through the story, deafening the terrified man, who is facing agony and death. He is ferociously

punished by Tolstoy for his conventional desires and his ego-
tism and for his refusal to admit to the triviality and therefore
the sinfulness of his life. The last-minute redemption – literally, a flash of light – is meant to reward him for the spasm
of pity and sympathy he suddenly feels for his family and for
the servants who have cared for him, though it is not dis-
cernible to those listening in horror to his rattling death
throes.

Chekhov must have read Tolstoy's *Ivan Ilyich* when, at
twenty-nine, he wrote *A Boring Story (From an Old Man's
Notebook)*. His old man is sixty-two and dying, but he still lectures as a medical scientist in the university, though no
longer, he feels, with flair and confidence. Chekhov imagined
a distinguished and intelligent old man who has lost his
appetite for almost everything and is now stranded without
what he thinks of as 'a ruling idea . . . and if that is not there,
nothing is there'. He wavers between a belief that he has
changed and the suspicion that he may always have been like
this, but simply not been aware of it. It is a frightening suspicion, harboured, I imagine, by many of us: the possibility
that we were never as quick or as talented or as charming as
we might have been or even remember being, that, indeed,
there has not been such a falling away, after all. But
Chekhov's old man knows, at least, that he has lost ground,
power, authority, and he even knows that he is compound-
ing the loss by hating the world around him:

I hate, I despise, I am filled with indignation. I am exasperated, and I am afraid. I have become quite excessively

strict, demanding, irritable, rude, suspicious . . . Has the world become worse? Have I become better? Or have I been blind and indifferent till now?

Just as he realises that he has lost his 'ruling idea' and that he can't live without it, he also confronts the horrifying reality that most people live their lives without such an idea, and that for some of them, particularly for his beloved adopted daughter Katya, this is a tragedy. There is also the possibility that he may never have had a 'ruling idea' himself: a possibility that the old have always to confront, at exactly the moment when they realise that it is too late to do anything about it. The story offers a compassionate commentary on Tolstoy's. There is no final flash of light, no last-minute escape from hellfire, but a credible intelligence grappling with its own collapse. Recognising one's own mental and moral deterioration is surely a remarkable human capability, and to have represented it in fiction, as Chekhov so movingly does, even more than that.

5

The Hospital Years

A statistic from nowhere, or nowhere I remember, but it has the ring of truth. If most of us can look forward to living for about ten years longer than our parents (which might, in my case, mean living to be a hundred or more) we can also expect to spend the equivalent of eight of those years in hospital or doctors' waiting-rooms. Gore Vidal left Italy for California recently, when his companion died and he himself was nearly eighty. When asked why, he spoke of his future as 'the hospital years', years which might be easier to live out in California.

My local hospital has become a cross between a garage and a shopping precinct. It contains not only shops and hairdressers and cafés, but every kind of human maintenance service for body, mind and soul. I suppose I should think myself lucky to have a large new hospital just behind my house, though I'm ashamed to admit that when its building was proposed I objected to it, even went to meetings to stop it all. It seemed too looming and ambitious for the small space it was meant to occupy. The building work started disarmingly with its own separate Aids clinic, one of the first in London, so that many of us protesters were instantly silenced. And then came the psychiatric unit, just behind our garden wall, from which issue occasional startling shouts and heart-rending wails. Now, nearly twenty years after it began, it is an important institution in this part of London, with its own bus stop: ugly on the outside and beautiful within, though both the outside and the inside seem differently determined to masquerade as something that is not a hospital. Its modern façade was meant to fit into the shops it sits among, and tucked into it are a post office, a café, a mobile phone shop and another shop that sells the unhealthiest snacks and fizzy drinks known to the Western world. Desperate smokers – patients on crutches, in wheelchairs and dressing-gowns, nurses, doctors, visitors – cough and cluster outside the elaborately revolving doors, which stall unforgivingly if you approach them with any verve.

Inside, however, there are constant and changing exhibitions of sculpture, pictures and mobiles. There are sales of books and cakes and unusual garments on most days of the week. The building itself is curiously ship-like, constructed to seem open to the sky. There are wards from which you might gaze out across the roofs of London with a telescope to one eye, and walkways like gangplanks and a chapel suspended in space, a kind of crow's nest from which to survey the turbulence below. As I lay recently in the anteroom to the theatre where the first of my knees was to be replaced I looked up at a ceiling dreamily adorned with wreaths and nymphs.

In this surprising building, I have now been in receipt of two new knees and weeks of physiotherapy in a hot pool and a gym. Twice a year I have my eyes tested for glaucoma and for mysterious 'Drusen' growths at the sides of my eyes, which must be stopped from putting pressure on the optic nerve. Almost all the eye specialists are beautiful, elegantly dressed women from the Indian subcontinent, who ask you to gaze at one of their earrings while they gaze into one of your eyes. Also twice a year I go less happily through the endoscopy department to emerge bloated and suffering after a 'procedure' I shall decently leave to the imagination. I have had X-rays of most bits of me and MRI scans, and tests for heart and lungs on a machine that simulates running uphill. I have been asked to count backwards in sevens and remember the name of the Prime Minister (this was part of a somewhat cursory test for Alzheimer's). Babies are born here and weighed and measured and tested for years to come. Stephen Ward – society portrait painter and osteopath, as well as haughty pander, the miscast rogue at the heart of the Profumo scandal of 1963, who killed himself and was, I suppose, its principal casualty – died here (though that was in this hospital's previous workhouse incarnation). The Accident and Emergency Department can seem on a late Saturday night to be a scene from a play by Ionesco, faked and drummed up, most of the time silent but for the occasional scream from a drunken peeress, rigid in top-to-toe tartan, or the burblings of bluff sportsmen and military men, whose weekends are not going well. Only my teeth fail to interest anyone in this glorious National Health galleon, and for their sorry state I travel by three forms of public transport to north London, sometimes once a week. All that doesn't quite add up to four-fifths of my life, but it is mounting up.

I'm not sure that this new familiarity with the inside of a large teaching hospital is especially cheering or enlightening, but it is, I think, intrinsic to contemporary experience. Philip Roth's book *Everyman* springs brilliantly out of the new knowingness – no doubt partial and amateurish, but full of relish for the language and the detail – that we all exhibit about disease and treatment and dying these days. No one will hold a mirror to our lips or pass a feather or a lighted candle before us to check whether we've died or not, and we'll be lucky to do it in our own beds. There will soon be no more jokes of the 'Doctor, I'm all pains' or 'something's up with her tubes' sort. Here, for instance, is Roth's hero talking on the telephone to the wife of his old friend, who died suddenly at home while she was out to lunch:

'Was it a stroke or was it a heart attack?' he asked her.

'It was a myocardial infarct.'

'Had he been feeling ill?'

'Well his blood pressure had been – well, he had a lot of trouble with his blood pressure. And then this past weekend he wasn't feeling so great. His blood pressure had gone up again.'

'They couldn't control that with drugs?'

Roth's unnamed hero, his Everyman, is understandably interested in the manner of his friend's dying. He probably owns his own blood-pressure gauge too, and 'not a year went by when he wasn't hospitalized'. We get the details: 'The year after he had carotid artery surgery he had an angiogram in which the doctor discovered that he'd had a silent heart attack on the posterior wall because of an obstructed graft.'

The novel starts with this man's funeral and ends with his death, which turns out to be 'just as he'd feared from the start'; and the saga of his operations or procedures, as they're often euphemistically called, runs alongside, in syncopated time, the saga of his failed marriages and his affairs, his bad relations with his sons and his less than heroic adventures. Meanwhile, his entirely healthy, successful and virtuous older brother Howie stands not just as a reproach but as possibly the instigator of, or even the inspiration for, his illnesses. He has believed all his life that he loved and admired Howie, but finally admits to himself that

he hated Howie because of his robust good health. He hated Howie because he'd never in his life been a patient in a hospital, because disease was unknown to him, because nowhere was his body scarred from the surgical knife, nor were six metal stents lodged in his arteries along with a cardiac alarm system tucked into the wall of his chest that was called a defibrillator, a word that when he first heard it pronounced by his cardiologist was unknown to him and sounded, innocuously enough, as if it had something to do with the gear system of a bicycle.

The hatred and the envy prey on him and make him iller. He is reminded of a time when his psychoanalyst insisted that his appendicitis was caused by envy, and perhaps it was. Not only that. It is as if a healthy old age is *morally* superior to its alternative, as if frailty in old age, whether physical or mental, is always all your own fault. Old people are often told they're 'marvellous' for simply being there and not complaining much. As though our longevity or our susceptibility to disease were entirely up to us, were choices we make: pain and illness the outward signs of weakness, vacillation, lack of character; health the well-earned consequence of courage and exactly the right amount of moral fibre. The man or woman who meekly submits to illness and death rather than 'fighting' it, 'putting up a struggle', is unlikely to figure gloriously in the obituary columns. It's all a far cry from Edith Wharton's grimly generic hypochondriac in *Ethan Frome*, who knows that she has finally got the upper hand in her marriage when she is able to announce triumphantly, 'I've got complications.' As Wharton points out, 'Almost everybody in the neighbourhood had "troubles", frankly localized and specified; but only the chosen had "complications".'

What are we allowed to say about pain? The hardest aspect of it is the difficulty of describing it, measuring it, knowing whether it is better or worse, more or less, than anyone else's or, indeed, our own on another day. On a scale of 1 to 10, we're asked. How do you know? I'd plump for 7 or 8, if only to keep up with the woman who has 'complications'. When a recent doctor's report from the endoscopy department included the words 'low pain threshold' I felt accused and slandered. How could he know that? How can any of us know? Perhaps the pain was beyond anyone's threshold. We'll never know. When footballers writhe with pain in the middle of a match, the commentators sometimes take it for granted that they're bluffing, though I find myself wincing in anguished sympathy with the pain they appear to be suffering, however formulaically acted out.

In Roth's novel, the hero runs a painting class for the old people he lives among. There is a talented widow who suffers atrocious back pain, wears a hard plastic brace and cries with shame as she admits to the pain and the brace. Not long after doing so, she kills herself with an overdose of sleeping pills. Does she have a 'low pain threshold'? Does she lack stamina? Is she ashamed of her pain, embarrassed by it? Then there is an advertisement on the buses at the moment, in which a man appears to have an extremely tight belt buckled across his nipples. It is meant to suggest the chest pain you would feel if you were having a heart attack or were about to. It is clearly well intentioned, but it leaves you with a puzzle. How do we know what his pain is like, let alone whether ours is like his? Would imagining his pain help me to recognise my own as somehow similar or different? All this is more important than it might seem since that sinister word 'triage' has been reintroduced into medical practice, reminding you of Florence Nightingale and her nurses patrolling the tents in the Crimea in order to decide which of the wounded were worth treating, which should be attended to first and which were not worth bothering about because they were bound to die anyway. It may no longer be wise to show fortitude under stress if we want our ailments to be taken seriously.

For instance, I woke up this morning with an ominous pain on the right side of my chest. There are some good things about new, sharp pains: they tend to blot out the older, more persistent ones. So, unusually, I had no cramp in my legs, nor could I feel the sharp agony and intractable stiffness in the small of my back (caused, I think, by spondylitis, and apparently exacerbated by rest) that greets me on other mornings. These receded, yielding to the competition of this exciting new pain. I lay in bed for a bit, imagining that I was going to have a heart attack, probably in the pool I swim in every morning, but just as probably on my walk there or, if I was luckier, on the way back. At least then I'd be able to gesture towards my home or even towards the hospital behind it to whoever might, or might not, choose to ask if I was in trouble. The pain hadn't gone when I had had breakfast, nor when I had read my three Russian pages of *Anna Karenina* (a difficult bit full of ploughs and harrows and furrows and several categories of farm labourer, but wonderful about Levin on the first day of spring, momentarily forgetting his woes and even recovering spontaneously from the crossness he'd felt at first that none of the winter jobs on the farm that he'd hoped would be done, had been done). Then I walked to swimming, did my twenty lengths and walked home. The pain was still there, but milder now.

Having survived those tests, I considered as I walked the possibility that what this pain signified was more likely to be lung cancer than heart disease, and I wondered for a bit whether or not I should have chemotherapy or surgery in that case and whom I might discourage from visiting me on my sickbed, since I absolutely don't want to be seen by just anybody when in pain and without hair or dizzy with morphine. I thought too for a little while, though inconclusively, about my funeral. Where it would be, and the music. There is Purcell's 'When I Am Laid in Earth', which would make people cry a bit, but would not be suitable, I suppose, if I'm cremated. Would someone say something nice about me without going in for the sort of funeral hyperbole that would deeply embarrass my children and my husband and my sisters, who know better and are inclined to take things 'with a pinch of salt'. And then there was the question of who wouldn't bother to come and who would come just because they were pleased I'd died or simply had a thing about going to funerals.

The pain was gone by the next morning, though by then I had another one, which could have emanated from my hip or, perhaps, if I was sure of their whereabouts, my kidneys. So almost every day I have a completely new pain. Then I had an agonising and disabling heel for two months, possibly caused by the lightest of leaps from one ancient boulder to another in the Fort of Tughlaqabad on the outskirts of Delhi. But then one morning I woke up and it had gone. I sometimes think that it isn't possible to have all that many pains at the same time because they vie for dominance and cancel each other out. I do sometimes report these mysterious pains to my kind doctor, who takes some of them quite seriously. But usually she has no explanation and nor have I. And there's not much point wondering whether these pains are imagined or whether I am a hopeless hypochondriac, because of course they are and of course I am; but so what? We live with the reality and this other reality and then there's the reality of doctors and tests and diagnoses. I believe it is customary to tell men who have just learned that they have prostate cancer that they are much more likely to die of something else. So they shouldn't worry unduly. I suppose that's meant to be a comfort, distracting you from the cancer and allowing your imagination to roam freely over all the other lethal possibilities which will outdo it, and you, in the end.

The pains of old age are often undiagnosed and perhaps undiagnosable. Since they are usually produced by the gradual, or occasionally sudden, wearing out of bits of our minds and bodies, they are often less frightening than new and inexplicable pains were in one's youth, because for the most part they don't herald serious illness or catastrophe but simply remind us of our general and increasing debility. The bad thing about them, however, is that by and large they are going to get worse. If I find it painful getting out of bed in the morning, I am likely to find it harder still in five years' time. And then you have to add that though that is undoubtedly so, it is also quite possible that you won't be there in five years' time. And given that it's pain you're thinking about, you're faced with a bit of a dilemma. Do you really *want* to be there having a much worse version of the pain that's bothering you now? Might it possibly be a relief not to be there?

But there was such a short bit of our lives when things weren't getting worse, when we could assume that change would be for the better, might even mean progress, that none of this is all that hard to get used to. The really difficult thing is this foreshortening of time. When Gore Vidal talks of 'the hospital years' he means his last years, not just a passing phase. And when we talk of our state of mind or health nowadays we probably aren't alluding to a temporary state, but to the present and the future and to a continuous, declining, but finite condition, and all of it hurtling along at great speed.

I should add that in fact I am in remarkably good health. I hardly ever get colds or flu. I can now walk for miles with my new knees and stand for quite long stretches at bus stops or in exhibitions. I will probably survive the boulders of Tughlaqabad if I visit them again. I hardly ever sleep in the daytime (but don't sleep nearly enough in the night) and I eat and drink as much and as indiscriminately as I ever did. (I can't, of course, vouch for my wits.) Not all my friends are so lucky. My main friend, indeed my husband of fifty-four years, for instance, has prostate cancer, deafening tinnitus in one ear, poor eyesight, a pacemaker that keeps him awake at night, bronchiectasis and high blood pressure and cholesterol. He too has spondylitis, which makes lying down painful and walking more so. He also has a hyper-sensitive knee, which he has long had, but which strives to keep up with the collection of parvenu pains he has acquired since. We compete on lots of fronts, but especially when it comes to pains and how to cure them. He is winning hands down at the moment on the pain front, though not the remedies, so that my musings on the subject refer to his life even more than they do to mine. And I haven't started on our rotting teeth and the interesting side-effects of all our pills and treatments or on what might be thought of as the ruder drawbacks we both suffer from, which are not always painful, though they are disagreeable and hard to live with.

My natural competitiveness let me down badly when I was assessed at the town hall for a temporary disability parking badge for my car. It was before I'd had my knees replaced, and I was having difficulty walking. There, in a tiny office, with an old-fashioned games teacher checking me for any tricks I might get up to, I found myself unable to resist showing her that I could still touch my toes, with my hands flat on the ground. Proving, I suppose, that I have long arms, short legs and little in the way of persuasive gifts. I was denied the badge.

I have once again been invited to join a focus group, and this time I have accepted. Clearly, we come in handy for such things, we retired old people. Though funnily enough I was braced to serve for the first time in my life on a jury a year or two ago when I received a second order, telling me that I was too old to do so. I think I might do quite well on a jury, so long as I wasn't in charge of it. In this focus group, five or six of us, who have spent more time than we can possibly have wanted to in the local Endoscopy Department, have been invited to discuss our experiences there. It is as if I'd got through an audition to play the part of Andromache 'sunk in misery' or Niobe 'all tears'. Will I be able to explain my wincing horror of it all and my fury at being thought to have a low pain threshold? Of course not. I shall be obliging and brave.

I suppose dying is going to be a harder matter. One of my friends joined EXIT some years ago. It is an organisation based in Scotland that promotes 'self-deliverance'. But her children found out about it and were horrified, and for several reasons she won't be availing herself of their helpful if somewhat ghoulish services. My old friend Anne Wollheim had a really bad month or two at the end of her life and was known to wonder aloud, 'Where is Dr Shipman now?' In fact, she had more than a year of knowing she was going to die and refusing to have the treatment which would probably not have lengthened her life by much. She filled that year with children and grandchildren and family and friends and travel, so that I find myself hoping that only the last two months or so were intolerable. But that was far too much, and it seemed barbaric that she couldn't decide when to die and how, and that her doctors couldn't openly help her. Yet so deep-seated is the horror of suicide that most of us are uncertain about the viability of legal euthanasia, especially when, as it usually does for the old, it involves someone else. And none of us is quite ready yet to stand in for Dr Shipman, who killed at least 215 of his old patients. If it is true that we have ten extra years of life nowadays, but that eight of them bear more than a shadow of decrepitude and the complicated moral choices inflicted on us by medical advances, we will need to work out how to get more control over the ways there may be of ending it all.

6

Time

There are days when the interval between drawing back the curtains in the morning and closing them in the evening is so short that it seems hardly worth acknowledging it as a day at all. By the time I've done my hour of *Anna Karenina*, reading it slowly in Russian with a dictionary and a translation nearby, and had my swim, it's almost lunchtime. Then there's the news and *Neighbours*. Days and weeks and years rush by, flipped and skimmed and barely read, like the pages of a book you're hurrying through to find something you half remember seeing there, without letting yourself become seriously interested in the book itself. As time speeds up, the future and its inevitable deteriorations get closer. Just as you become slower at everything you do, take longer to do the simplest things, you find yourself hurtling downhill with no brakes.

So much of my youth was spent waiting for things. Five minutes of waiting and you thought you'd die of it, and a year ahead was unimaginable. Sundays were boring and interminable, and I still can't get used to the idea that you can shop and do things on Sundays that are not going for a walk: Sundays are meant to be boring. I realised the other day that my grandfather was old during all the time I knew him, and that from sixty to eighty-one, when he died, time must have been rattling by for him, when it was hardly moving at all for me. But perhaps those were the best years of his life. He was thought to be a much better grandfather than father, after all; and his younger daughter, my Aunt Esther (the encouraging Auntie Jezebel of my youth), who was a singer and a teacher of singers, was known for having a much better time in her old age than she had in her youth. Her mother's death when she was ten, her hatred of the various schools she was sent to, her father's suspicion of any man who showed an interest in her, an uncomfortable marriage — all these faded to insignificance when she gathered glory as a teacher in her fifties and sixties and went on to have lovers and admirers and a brilliant and honoured old age until she was ninety-two.

Even when I was grown up and my children were babies, I longed for them to grow up (foolishly, it seems now), mostly out of curiosity. They seemed to take a long time doing so at first, and then this new breathless, rushing time set in for me, and suddenly they were not only not babies, they were having sex and babies themselves, and jobs and partners and houses and complicated and difficult lives and even some grey hair, while I had tipped over into this accelerated descent towards the end.

And all that waiting I went in for was for things that might be good, after all, might make life better in some way, might constitute progress. We were told and learned to tell ourselves to be patient. It takes time. Everything takes time. Patience means almost nothing now that we know for certain that things will get worse, and, what's more, sooner rather than later; and I, at least, want more than anything to slow it all down, to savour what is still good now, to make our time coincide with the time lived by the young, which stretches so unendingly for them and for which they have so little respect. Patience is not what we need.

I first read Frank Kermode's *The Sense of an Ending* more than forty years ago, and I remember being drawn to his playful illustration of the time that a plot in a novel must somehow account for. 'The clock's *tick-tock* I take to be a model of what we call a plot, an organization that humanizes time by giving it form; and the interval between *tock* and *tick* represents purely successive, disorganized time of the sort that we need to humanize.' He goes on, 'It is not that we are connoisseurs of chaos, but that we are surrounded by it, and equipped for co-existence with it only by our fictive powers.' I thought then that he was saying something profound about literature, as he was. He was also saying something about how we think and talk about our lives. Not only do we arrange the whole of human history into centuries, epochs, periods, decades. We do the same with our own lives. There's the bit, for instance, before

memory really starts, our prehistory, recallable archaeo-
logically through photographs, stories we're told, when our
parents were young and wore clothes we don't remember
seeing. I peer into their handsome faces, arranged shyly and
blandly for the photographer, giving nothing away and never
off-guard, as I remember them. That's the bit I've wanted to
recover in my old age: my own beginnings, of course, but
also my parents' youth, their lives before I knew them. Then
there's the first remembering, which comes to me, at any
rate, in vivid, disconnected flashes, isolated moments, clear
and dreamlike and sorely in need of fictive ordering and
explanation, which their sudden and incomplete character
seems to demand: particular buildings, a wet pavement; an
ice-cream seller in a blue and white uniform, standing by
the box on the front of his bicycle, and the green and red
Bakelite tubs with a miniature wooden spoon you could buy
from him; a girl handing over a shilling in a dairy (there are
no such shops any more), who is asked her age and proudly,
impressively, announces that she is ten, an age I knew to be
both unattainable and roughly twice my own. A visit from
our rollicking German doctor when I was in bed with what
seems to have been a TB gland and his rolling r's as he re-
commended that I be fed on raspberries. I had difficulty
pronouncing my r's when I was a child, for which I was
teased, and I cured myself by endless whispered practising.
Why do I remember these few brightly lit moments and so
little in between, except sometimes the traces of excitement, fear, anxiety that the moments themselves may
possibly contain and even stand for? Though in fact the

strongest emotions I remember from childhood are shame and embarrassment. And all those memories are old ones anyway, often returned to, probably honed and buffed over the years, no longer involuntary or startling.

The long years between youth and old age, most of it reduced by memory to tock-tick time, may occasionally be organised in relation to moments of change, even crises. As Kermode puts it, 'We hunger for ends and for crises', if only to signpost and separate out those long stretches of time that are chiefly remembered for what was habitual, regular, repeated, monotonous: Mondays to Fridays and then the inevitable disappointment of weekends. But I do remember quite a lot of things before that. For instance, suddenly, when I was eleven, I knew everything and knew that I knew everything. I think this omniscience lasted for less than a week, but for those few days I underwent something like an out-of-body experience. I remember feeling heavy with knowledge. I was certain of what I knew and concerned and even worried that no one else knew it too, or, if they did, were not disposed to say so. What I knew seemed to me so distinctive and complete that it would have been very difficult for anyone else to possess that knowledge as I possessed it. I don't think I got any particular pleasure from my sudden omniscience, nor can I remember what additional item of knowledge had so decisively tipped the balance. I also worried that life might become intolerably dull from now on: no surprises or new satisfactions, and there would be little point in talking to anyone else, since they knew so much less than I did, and there was, therefore, little or nothing to be gained from that. And then what was I to do with the rest of my life? My apogee, as it were, had been reached, and there was nothing more to learn, find out, see, hear or want. I remember briefly envying everyone I knew who was younger than I was: their innocence, their ignorance and their possibilities were states of mind, conditions I'd lost and would never recover. And this was before I'd even acquired breasts and when my face was still as round as an apple.

Now I know practically nothing at all. Everything that I do know swims in a flush of ignorance, about which, at least, I *am* clear. So that nowadays, if I feel a disquisition coming on me I hold back, I even stutter, for fear that at the crunch moment, the particular name or word on which my story or case or argument depends will suddenly fly out of my head (and forgetting does feel like flight, and then as if the lost word or thought is hovering, tantalisingly, moth-like, just out of reach), only to be retrieved by accident some hours later as I am walking back from swimming or the postbox, and thinking about something quite different. I have just had to ask my grandson for the word 'tattoo'. I got it from him by miming David Beckham's arms and the back of his neck, and the patterns on them. And 'moussaka', which I lost this morning and had to replace with 'lasagna', has miraculously returned to me as I write and have no use for it. Other words that regularly escape me are 'nectarine' and 'agapanthus'. But people's names fly off most often. My mind often feels like an overflowing wastepaper basket, full of the last two-thirds of radio programmes, whose announced subject-matter and authors I have managed to miss, and shadowy

scraps of information picked up from the World Service
during insomniac nights.

Everything I've learned since I was eleven and knew
everything – about India, say, or ironing a shirt, or Russian,
or driving, or feminism, or having babies, or much later, for
that matter, being a grandmother; or about the inequities and
barbarisms of the British education and tax systems – has
come with its own built-in reminder that my experience is
not to be generalised and that I must regard myself as lodged
somewhere on the very lowest foothills of these topics. That,
I think, is the main advantage conferred by a long and costly
education: a relatively clear sense of what one doesn't know
and can't understand and never will. So that when I read
Bernard Williams discussing the possibility that eternal life,
were it in prospect, might profitably be 'occupied in something like intense intellectual enquiry', and then arguing
with Stuart Hampshire's view of the matter – which was,
apparently, that 'in pure intellectual activity the mind is most
free because it is then least determined by causes outside its
immediate states'– I am confronted with the thought that I
have never gone in for intellectual activity of quite that sort,
or rather that, if I have for a moment or two, I have delib-
erately interrupted myself in order not to get too hopelessly
out of my depth. Anyway, I can't imagine having a serious
think without doing something else at the same time: listening to music, doing a crossword or a sudoku, say, some
mending or ironing, filing my nails. And that may interfere
with the thinking.

*

I find it difficult to detach myself sufficiently from the times I've lived through in order to marvel properly at the changes that have characterised them. I'm always a little offended by black and white photographs of children in the thirties, or by old films and newsreels. The children look so shabby and oppressed; their games and interests so antediluvian. I feel loyal to the decade of my childhood, and I know that we thought of ourselves as canny and streetwise and cool, even if we weren't. I was good at jacks and skipping and juggling, activities that took me into the street and were predictably discouraged as mindless and a waste of time and effort by my parents; rather as parents, nowadays, worry about time spent on computers or watching television. Nonetheless, I knew these things were what mattered. Doesn't every generation? I have the sense that I swaggered a bit as I climbed trees and rode my bicycle with no hands and put up with my unforgivably girlish shorts. But our floppy hair ribbons and passed-down dresses with their let-down hems, our Fair Isle jerseys and the boys' short-back-and-sides and hopelessly long shorts, make us oddities now, sometimes even to ourselves. I've been reading a novel by Sarah Waters that starts off a bit later, in 1947, and she brilliantly catches the smells, the sights, the slang that I remember. But what a sorry lot we seem, putting up with permed hair and lino and tinned ham, with houses left like solitary teeth in bombed London terraces. But the sun shone for us too, and at fifteen you could be as oblivious to postwar rubble as to more everyday forms of shabbiness.

It is also true that I am still astonished to see people

apparently talking to themselves as they walk down the street alone or sit in buses babbling into their mobiles about where they've reached and when they're likely to be home. Nor will I ever get used to being able to communicate so easily with people in India or America by email or fax or phone. We used to make trunk calls once a year (if at all) to friends in France, and sometimes you had to book calls in advance. And as Stefan Zweig put it, 'a trunk call doesn't give one time to mince matters'. Such calls were thought of as exorbitantly expensive and therefore, as they were measured by the second, unsatisfactorily short. I remember telegrams and the post office, where someone behind a wire grid would help you cut the words of your message to a mini-mum in order to save money. Being able to construct a succinct telegram seemed the only advantage to be had from learning to do a précis in English lessons. And despite all the trouble you took with your telegram you knew that most of the time your message would reach its destination only if someone at the other end was ready to pedal like mad to get it there.

When I got married I had no car, no fridge, no washing-machine, no dishwasher, no central heating, no vacuum cleaner, no toaster, no television, no shower and no record-player. (I did have an enormous wireless, inherited from my grandfather and made of reddish varnished mahogany.) I don't think I thought of these as negatives or lacks. In fact, I thought my life rather easy and modern and a good deal more comfortable than my parents'. Slowly we acquired those things, so that now it is hard to imagine living without most of them or the other essentials that have been added since. So I have lived through the years in which those things stopped being luxuries and became essential for most people living in this country. Perhaps there are ways in which I am marked by that transition. I am a more awkward and frightened user of my computer and my microwave oven and my mobile phone than my grandchildren are, and I suppose they can look forward to even faster and more shocking changes of that sort, and it may be that they are braced for them as I was not.

It is not surprising that memory comes to seem vital to us in old age, such a touchstone. Not only are we threatened with losing it, and with all that that entails, it can also seem to be the only guarantor of our having been here at all. In *Patrimony* Philip Roth writes about his father that 'To be alive, to him, is to be made of memory – to him if a man's not made of memory, he's made of nothing.' Yet memory is so erratic and unreliable in most of what it delivers from the past, so partisan, so vulnerable to imagination, so malleable, that if we look to it to deliver what we ask of it, it usually fails. At its best it seems to function in an involuntary or undetectable way, as something like an extension of our nerves and blood and senses, yielding up pictures, scenes, a kind of newsreel of images and events, though rarely on demand. I am especially puzzled by the fact that memory is so much better at unhappiness than happiness.

Almost the only sententious moment in the whole of *Anna Karenina* is that famous first line: 'All happy families resemble one another, but each unhappy family is unhappy in its own way.' Tolstoy must have added it later or used it to get started, and he was perhaps right about families; though, unlike almost every other single thing he tells us in the novel, it doesn't really seem worth saying. But he was right about happiness. It isn't all that interesting to read about and it seldom seems to be memorable. What is there to be said about it? I think of it as the default position, the norm, the state other states diverge from, fitfully or constantly, mildly or seriously. But it is those shifts from the norm that we seem to remember more easily.

This is my fifth reading of *Anna Karenina*, the first in Russian, the first marvellously slow tasting of it, and sometimes I feel that I never want to read anything else. Though it is written in the past tense, as you'd expect, each scene seems to be happening as Tolstoy is writing it and sometimes even as we're reading it, as if he were watching it and listening in at that very moment. Everything we learn about the characters and their lives spins out from the detail and particularity of these scenes as they are happening. Moments of happiness are recorded as surprising, fleeting, physically registered moments, alternating with and sometimes accompanying feelings of shame, rage, disappointment, embarrassment. You can't imagine Tolstoy making much use of the pluperfect (which doesn't really exist in Russian, anyway), because he hardly ever bothers with his characters' past: a rare short paragraph tells us that Karenin was an orphan or that Anna was married off by an aunt and was always kind to her servants. But there is no sense of Tolstoy urgently packing in information about the past so that we'll understand what's going on in the present. At the end, when Anna is rushing through Moscow to the railway station and her death, she remembers moments from her youth for the first time in the novel. But there's nothing about her childhood, when as brother and sister, Anna and Stepan Oblonsky presumably lived together in the same house.

People in the novel live in their bodies and minds, and almost all the time it is their current consciousness that we're given, what they're thinking and feeling during the events and conversations of a particular scene. These scenes very rarely include Tolstoy's views of his characters' actions and behaviour, though of course he manages to let you know that he disapproves of Anna despite loving her, at least to begin with, and knowing that she couldn't help doing what she did, and that he doesn't like Vronsky. His bald patch and his belief in himself as a seriously promising painter give Tolstoy's dislike of him away. Tolstoy, who probably had more hair than he really needed, makes a good deal out of baldness in his novels. Infinitesimal vanities do give people away: long and carefully tended nails, for instance, tell the tale for Tolstoy here. If he doesn't spend much time on his characters' memories, he spends much more on their dress, their gestures, their fidgeting. Who can forget Karenin's lawyer catching moths while trying not to laugh at poor Karenin's sorry tale of cuckoldry? This is how we encounter and think of other people, caught up in moments which can seem to contain their whole lives, their complete personalities:

Vronsky on the day of the races, for instance, or Levin on the day when he is overcome with jealousy of the plump, fashionable, handsome young man-about-town Oblonsky has brought to stay, got up in a tartan bonnet with streaming ribbons. Levin is instantly convinced that Kitty must be in love with this obnoxious stranger.

Tolstoy seems to be telling us that people's pasts and their memories of the past are not separate from their present selves, are not some bran-tub from which they may, if they choose, retrieve unpredictable as well as predictable moments. Rather, the past and memories of it are incorporated into their bodies and lives and thoughts and actions. So Vronsky's hectic behaviour on the day of the races and Levin's hatred of his handsome visitor carry the past and memories of it, just as they contribute to their futures. You could say simply that we watch them behave 'in character', and that this inevitably contains aspects and memories of the past. Similarly, Kitty's memories of making jam in her own home as a girl are there as part of her, activated for us at the moment when she offends Levin's old nurse Agafya by refusing to make jam in the way it has always been made in the Levin household, by adding water to the syrup. The memory is invoked for Kitty by Agafya's sulking, and that moment enables Tolstoy to suggest the different worlds inhabited by Levin and Kitty before their marriage and the strain this sometimes puts on them now.

But none of that explains why it should be easier to remember unhappiness than happiness. It is not only that I remember weeping and despairing and feeling ill from sleeplessness and shedding too many tears; though I can no longer work my way back into most of the events and moods and quarrels and fears that produced all that misery. It's just the misery I remember. And curiously I can see myself in those scenes of misery. I don't as a rule appear in my own memories. I am there in most of them only as a disembodied spectator, the one having the memory rather than an actor in it. But in my sad memories I can sometimes see my body, if not my face. In one memory, for instance, I am wearing a tight, rather elegant Biba dress, dark, reddish purple, with a swirly skirt and long, narrow sleeves with witch-like points over the wrists, and pointed and slightly sinister boots, also from Biba, of the same colour. And I am looking at myself in the narrow mirror on the front of a heavily varnished orange-coloured wardrobe in the house we rented for a time in the Scottish Borders, a wardrobe I bought for five pounds from the Salvation Army in Edinburgh. Can it be that I was watching myself at the time? Was I actually looking in the mirror to see what I looked like in a state of misery? Was I somehow detached and yet interested in the fact that I was unhappy, and must therefore be looking and behaving like someone who was unhappy? Or perhaps I wasn't behaving as an unhappy woman is expected to behave and was embarrassed by that fact.

It seems much more difficult to recall strong emotion than to remember how you behaved in response to it. I do remember that I often felt I lived a double life. No one at school or university or, later, at work, nor in our local Scottish village, would ever have guessed that I wept so much. And when I think now about that double life I don't understand it. I don't know what the inhabitant of one of those lives thought about the inhabitant of the other one. And now, nearly forty years later, I am heiress to both lives, both selves, and not entirely certain that I know either of them.

I would like to be able to say that I remember being happy in the same way. And I do have little sparks and whiffs of remembering that too, though there are no brightly dressed bodies or grinning faces to bear me out. The feelings seem from here to be more like relief than bliss. Sighs of satisfaction that I was suddenly not anxious or tired or angry. That kind of sighing seems mostly to have happened in the countryside or the bath. But there are good urban memories too, which usually contain surprises, and I have learned to summon them up. I have for years engineered a return moment of bliss on about the 12th of April when I catch the first pale-purple flower bursting out of the side of its bud on a nearby Paulownia tree; and the births of my babies, the moments when they first appeared in the world, I remember as unadulterated happiness. The arrival of an entirely new human being, who has never existed before, is surely a miraculous compensation for the everlasting absence that a death announces.

It is not, I should quickly add, that I think of myself as having had an unhappy life. Quite the opposite. I've been lucky in almost every respect. Those long years of adulthood, of having children and working, were good ones for me. But memory has made them seamless, unchanging, devoid of crises. And if I try to plant some markers in them, if only for organisational purposes, they usually turn out to be bad ones.

But that's not to say that the continuous, the repeated, the tock-tick years are to be sniffed at. I have lived in the same house for fifty years. When we originally considered buying a forty-year lease on it for a little over £6000, we were warned by our lawyer and our bank manager that we were taking a serious risk, would have difficulty getting a mortgage and might, if we did, given our likely employment possibilities, find it difficult to pay off. We were lent more than a third of the price by family and friends, and within a year or two, because of inflation, paying off the £4000 mortgage and then the debt had become quite easy. And all this in Chelsea, which was not quite so full of bankers and pop stars as it is today, but seemed well above our station even then.

Chelsea is one half of the Royal Borough of Kensington and Chelsea, and my bit of it, World's End, is at its southwestern tail. When we moved into this small white terraced house in the summer of 1960 we were told by the plumber, who had lived in a nearby street as a child before the war, that this was a bad area, a satellite colony of Fulham's infamous scrap-metal trade and full of extremely dodgy customers. Charles Booth had it marked on one of his demographic maps of London as populated by the criminal classes. If it was, it is no longer. Though now I come to think of it, it probably still is. It is just that the criminal classes

dress differently these days, and I am saddled with a Dicken-
sian idea of what they ought to look like and how they
should behave. In those days our status as Chelsea residents
was often queried. Weren't we giving ourselves airs? This
wasn't the real Chelsea. It was Fulham. Even in Bombay I
was once reminded that I lived at the wrong end of the
King's Road. The ten-acre square of streets within which I
live is now thoroughly gentrified, and the houses we and our
neighbours all bought then for £6000 on forty-year leases
are now worth a good deal more than a million pounds each
for the freeholds we managed to acquire cheaply in the early
seventies. Since I am writing this in the very week that the
financial crash of 2008 has, it is hoped, reached its nadir, that
may no longer be true. From being the street's youngest and
riskiest inhabitants, we have become its oldest, and we are
no doubt a bit of a drug on the market for the entrepre-
neurial couples who buy up our neighbours' houses now,
then disappear while a team of builders from Eastern
Europe moves in for a year of transformation. We sit reading amidst the drilling and the demolition, our ears plugged
with wax.

The municipal swimming-pool was always there, halfway
down the King's Road and just behind the town hall and the
library. Nowadays, it is managed for the borough by a private
firm, but otherwise it is unchanged. It is seedy and charming and at no risk, it seems, of being modernised. Our
children learned to swim in it, and in those days I cheered
them for their lengths and their dives, from the wooden spec-
tators' benches on its wrought-iron balcony. But I rarely

joined them. I had been rather an ace swimmer at school, but when my children swam in the pool I watched rather than swam. I think I didn't want to get my hair wet. Now I swim every morning, and I walk there and back. I try to vary my journey, but there isn't much choice. I can walk through Carlyle Square and admire its Paulownia tree in springtime, and its huge leaves like an elephant's ears in late summer. Or I can remind myself that the gay men's shirt shop near my house (or the shop next to it) was once a butcher's, and that in order to visit our friends who lived in the flat above it, we had to force our way between enormous beef carcasses, pushing them aside like heavily beaded curtains in the door-way of some Eastern souk. There were one or two cottages with front gardens full of poppies and delphiniums on the King's Road when we moved in, and an old Dutch barn served as a builder's yard in a side-street.

Walking to swimming and back is still a pleasure, though it often rains and the traffic jams in the King's Road poison us pedestrians with their stinking fumes. For a time, I couldn't manage the walk because of arthritic knees. Then I learned to do it with a stick. Now I power along in all weathers, only a little unreliable, in my hideous MBT trainers (they come with a video teaching you how to walk in them). I am propelled by habit, perhaps also by a sort of addiction to exercise and the outdoors and the hoped-for rewards for virtue. This makes me happy. Once in the pool I am fifteen again, or I was before I had to give up breast stroke to save my replaced knees, which apparently have a life expectancy more limited even than my own. So my twenty lengths are a little more exhausting now than they used to be. In spite of its lanes full of children and their pee and peeled-off plasters, the silky water buoys me up. I am slower than I like to think I am, but my lengths don't tire me out as much as walking does, and as I swim my three different strokes I am, momentarily, a match for anyone.

I come down to earth in the changing-room, though I am nothing like as old as some of my fellow swimmers: indeed, I am still a girl to some of them. There is the beautiful ninety-year-old, who modelled hats for Aage Thaarup, walks on air and has a back as straight as an ironing-board. She speaks sadly of her equally beautiful friend, who gave up swimming last year: too much tripping and toppling and black eyes, and she now walks, exasperated, with a stick. The lanky, girlish widow of the designer of London Transport posters during the war, and of Penguin book covers and advertisements for Mac Fisheries after it, must be eighty or so. We know each other's first names and a lot about each other. Indeed, the sort of intimacy that develops makes asking for second names rather difficult. We know each other's bodies and histories and children and long-ago jobs too well for that, but only a few of these friendships translate into the world outside.

Swimming has occupied the tock-tick part of my life and has lasted me well, connecting me with childhood while delivering its friendships and rituals in old age. I sometimes think that my local swimming-pool would be an ideal spot for dying. I could just expire, face down, doing my stately crawl. I suppose they'd have to close the pool for an hour or two and pretend they were cleaning it. Perhaps it would be simpler still to swim out to sea from Birling Gap. In *Coda*, the book Simon Gray wrote when he was dying, he ended one chapter with the words, 'I wish there were a way of just dissolving in the sea, without having to go through the business of drowning first.'

7

The Young and the Old

Occasionally, and I'm not sure why, I tell my granddaughters that I used to be rather a whizz at cartwheels and backbends and the Charleston, or that even though I became an English teacher I hated English at school until I was in the sixth form. They are perfectly polite about these items of information, but their eyes don't exactly light up, and occasionally they roll them a little sadly, or perhaps ironically. They don't set my news alongside their own, and the information certainly doesn't do the job I wanted it to do. This was, I think, to suggest that we have more in common than they might suppose, that I was once their age, that I had a childhood too and that I remember a fair amount about it, and that my childhood is there for me, in my head, even now, and that I could tell them more about it if they wanted me to. I found my twelve-year-old diary the other day, and thought of showing it to my twelve-year-old granddaughter. But I think it would confirm her view that we were all a bit 'lame' and far too easily satisfied. I seemed to find everything that happened to me 'nice' or even 'lovely', and I don't think that would do at all these days. Nor would the fact that my spelling was a bit better than most of theirs meet with much approval.

I suppose we're all bursting with stories from childhood, longing for the questions that will unlock them, release them into the world. When one of my granddaughters was doing the Second World War in History there was a moment when I became a useful source of information for her. I responded with a welter of evacuees and ration books and air-raid shelters and the blackout and dried eggs and years of living without oranges or bananas. Her teacher even thanked me for some of my offerings, which were added to the class archive on the subject, rather as birds' eggs or rare wild flowers may be added to the nature table. But I knew all the time that my granddaughter could have got most of all this from books or the Internet, and that the bits I really remembered, the stories in which I figured, were too idiosyncratic for the classroom or for her and would be hard to communicate in digestible form.

It ought, in principle, to be easier for the old to understand the young than for the young to understand us. We've been there, after all, and they haven't been where we are yet. But I'm not sure that it works like that. So much of our understanding of other people, particularly other much younger people, is done through memory, analogy, comparison. I think of myself as understanding my granddaughters more easily than my grandsons. But the truth is that their being girls doesn't really mean that I understand them – it simply means that I rummage more comfortably in my own memories for moments, feelings, events that might help me to understand them. And they, to do them justice, do the same thing in reverse. Our gender is invoked as one kind of bond. They give me advice about mascara and what I'm doing wrong on my computer. We discuss shampoo and smells and shopping. We inhabit the same world, but our heads are filled with such entirely different stories about it. Theirs contain (among much else) Beyoncé and Vampire books and parties and what, I think, are called social-networking sites. On these they cultivate the most intimate friendships, talking, writing, peering into each other's bedrooms on screen, though it seems that when they actually meet some of these hundreds of friends in the real world, as it were, they usually have nothing to say to each other, either because they've already said it all, or because the virtual is a good deal more conducive to confession and sympathy than reality is.

Identifying with people because they are girls or women never really works, yet it is something I continue to do against all the evidence. I should know by now that it is a mistake. I remember assuming that my teenage sons would become alien creatures from their puberty onwards and that I would continue to recognise my daughter at every point in her life. But it isn't necessarily like that, of course. Contemplating my two tall and beautiful grandsons, I am struck, as I was when their fathers were growing up, by the sheer difficulty of becoming an adult man. The girls do it all within a much firmer culture. They are surer of the rules and get more support from one another. There are difficulties about that, of course. It may be harder for girls to experiment or to stray from the conventional. But the demands on boys and the expectations of them seem contradictory and disconcerting. They are encouraged to develop self-sufficiency but also expected to master a sociability that girls enter and get the hang of much earlier and more easily.

Sometimes I'm possessed by my memories of being young: the houses I've lived in, the views from their windows, the road I used to take to school, the woods where we went on 'wet runs' on rainy days, the boy I had a 'pash' on (though 'pash' was my mother's name for it, not mine) and even what that felt like. I can live all over again moments of red-hot embarrassment and the efforts I made to brazen them out. I can recall the faces of almost everyone I knew as a child and reel off most of their names, but these days remembering the face of someone I've met in the morning is pretty well impossible by teatime. Yet I can see the thin whip-like branch that struck me in the face as I ran through the wood more than sixty years ago and which I turned round to examine and excoriate. But even as I remember moments, glimpses and even some habitual activities, these memories seem always to stand in a kind of syncopated relation to what's happening to my grandchildren now. And the colours and rhythm of my memories are dimmer, duller, faded, next to their lives, which present themselves, even to me, in sharp, clear outlines and strong primary colours.

The simplest words trip you up. You think you're agreeing or that you're agreeing to differ, but the differences in the meanings of words are likely to be differences of much more than words. For instance, in my day you 'went with' a boy. You might be asked if you were 'going with' a boy or if you wanted 'to go' with a boy. Now you 'go out with' a boy. Admittedly, I went to a boarding-school in the country and my grandchildren live in London and go to large comprehensive schools. The 'out' part of it all was bound to present difficulties. One of my granddaughters was exasperated that the boy she was 'going out' with wouldn't actually ask her to 'go out' with him. I think she meant that though they had arranged to go to a film together he hadn't declared himself. But it may have been the other way round: that they were in some kind of acknowledged relation to one another, but hadn't yet stepped out hand in hand, as it were, into the world. In the end she chucked him for prevarication and being smaller (if only temporarily) than she was. Both perfectly good reasons, I suppose, but I'm still not sure what his cardinal deficiency was, or what 'going out with' is meant to entail and does entail.

When that same granddaughter plays the violin at a concert, and so much better than I ever did, I am instantly and gloomily back waiting for my music lesson sixty years ago and listening to my teacher's young prodigy having her lesson before me, playing the Bach unaccompanied Chaconne in her white socks and Clarks sandals. Yet the apparent parallel or similarity is misleading. The two scenes don't match. My granddaughter looks cool and extraordinary as she plays her difficult pieces, a Cleopatra in plimsolls. Her playing classical music at all is a complicated declaration about what can be thought of as 'cool' if you make it so and if you are generally in credit on that score, as she seems to be. I was never cool enough in my own eyes because I knew nothing about popular music, partly because my parents despised it all, whatever it was, without actually hearing any or knowing anything about it. So now it's a struggle to keep those two moments, sixty years apart, separate and yet a pair that might somehow illuminate one another. We are and always have been out of step, not grossly so – that's the trouble – but slightly, almost imperceptibly; and every effort I make to understand these young human beings has to be tempered by this adjusting inner eye, this metronome, reminding me that there's something I can never know about being young now, and that my granddaughters can hardly help seeing my childhood in sepia tones, fixed and blurred by the bad snapshots people took in those days, by our 'lame' clothes and their perfunctory history lessons. Not quite a cacophony, but a dissonance, a mismatch. We are always slightly out of sync. But I've just been directed by one of them to something called 'The Urban Dictionary' on the Internet. Perhaps that will solve my problems.

I'm not sure that teenagers had been invented when I was of an age to be one. If they had been, they were some strange American phenomenon we didn't know much about. I remember those tartan Bermuda shorts and long socks and brown leather shoes with a coin tucked into them. They had button-down collars and T-shirts and Shetland sweaters. All this was enviable in some way, but foreign and bold and not for us. My kind Auntie Jezebel brought me a pair of

wonderful light-blue Wrangler jeans from America, however, which I wore with pride and delight. C&A was the
Primark of our day, and there you could buy cheap clothes
that differed in no obvious way from the clothes worn by
your mother and your aunts or, indeed, your grandmother;
though if you were a debutante you might wear pretty white
tulle on special occasions, and I was no debutante.

I suspect that one way or another all my grandchildren
are 'cool'. Not only that, they are cool 24/7, as they might
hideously put it. They have also been known to claim that
they'd much rather die than fail on any of the endlessly
proliferating criteria available to them for being cool. I
assume that they haven't thought seriously about what
dying involves, but perhaps they have. Maybe any potential
for embarrassment really is as serious as that, worth dying
to avoid. I hope not. Of course, we too were an embarrassment to ourselves, and to our elders – neither fish nor fowl,
at that age – though there was very little in the culture that
was meant especially for us, and I remember class as a far
more significant regulator of style than youth. I certainly don't
remember there being this up-to-the-minute international
network, or any of the strict cultural self-monitoring
exercised by the young, that there seems to me to be now.
Though that could be the skewed vision of an old person,
who is sometimes rendered weary, sceptical, ill at ease by the
speed of change and the complexity of young people's lives.
Perhaps it really does afford nothing but pleasure, this learning of the rules and deciding how to live by them, this sense
the young must sometimes have of belonging to a worldwide

movement that demands a good deal of them. But how painful it must be for those among them who can't or don't manage to join; and there must be as many of them as there ever were.

If my own children's childhood took a long time, their children seem to have unfurled into their distinctive selves in a split second. It's not just breasts and moustaches. Their growing-up has been like those magical Japanese paper flowers you could buy in a cockle-shell, put in a glass of water, and there, suddenly, was a tiny and elaborate bouquet of waving petals. I watched one of my granddaughters emerge from her mother, battleship grey and an infant stand-in for ET. She is now a five-foot-ten marvel and a stunning example of these alien creatures I am transfixed by. How has she learned in so short a time, I wonder, to do and be all the things young women have to do and be? How, more amazingly still, has she evolved into this unique person, uncopying and uncopiable, like no one who has ever existed before or ever will again, while also learning (sometimes painfully and extravagantly) just what is expected of her in the world she inhabits, just how like everyone else she must at least pretend to be? It is always an extraordinary performance, this growing-up. So speedy and efficient in some ways, despite its terrifying pitfalls. And this time round, with my grandchildren, I have watched the process from a privileged position, barely called upon to urge the business forward, nor blamed for its hiccups and slippages.

I remember my first sight of my first grandchild. The

nurses had tactfully placed a green cap on him because he
had emerged from his mother's womb with a head even
more like an egg than most babies' heads. By the next day
that astonishing peak at the top of him had disappeared, and
no cap was needed to persuade his grandmother of his
exceptional qualities. I'd have to say that during the speeded-
up twenty-one years of his life there were one or two
moments when I have wondered how it is that relatively few
parents give up on their children during their sullen teenage
years, when everything 'sucks': adults, Shakespeare, long
words, school. A controversy has been raging recently about
the reaction of his parents (who are writers) to a young man
who has, for three years or so, terrorised his family while
under the influence of a particularly damaging kind of mar-
ijuana, called skunk. His parents ejected him at one point
from the family home. I suppose that such a young man
would have been sent off to the army or the colonies in the
old days. The intensity of the public outcry over the issue is
due above all to his mother's having written a book about his
misdeeds and his parents' dilemma in relation to them. She
ignored or forgot that there is always an absolute embargo
on parents, especially mothers, writing about their children,
except winsomely or boastfully; though parents, and especially mothers, could be said to be the meat and potatoes of
psychoanalysis and of a million novels in which childhood
and parents are blamed for all manner of later misfortune.

What never sucked for my grandson, I should add, was his
burning sense of justice, a passionate politics, and music, and
I am enchanted by the anomalies of his style these days. As

a stern young anarchist he has assembled a magically recycled wardrobe from charity shops, which turns him into something between Trabb's boy in *Great Expectations* ('Don't know yah!') and a scion of the upper classes as they used to dress when I was twenty: in waistcoats, flat caps and a British Warm overcoat. Almost the only thing I have to say against him is that he doesn't read novels much and hasn't, therefore, met Bazarov in Turgenev's *Fathers and Sons* and been warned by him of the perils of dogmatism. I am so accustomed to using novels and their characters to explain what I mean that conversing with a young man who prefers to read Immanuel Kant, Noam Chomsky and Euripides is a bit as if we had no common language.

We agree about many things, but not about money. He, a poor student, heavily in debt, would like money to be abolished. Whereas I remember the pleasure I felt when I was first paid for something I'd done, something that, however minimally, was valued, thought useful in the world, worth paying for. It may well be a coincidence, but my other grandson has a tendency to divest himself of all that he owns: phones, cameras, garments, money float from him like leaves from a tree in October, and the taller he grows, the further his head is from the ground – and the distance increases by about six inches a year – the less he appears to want from the world. It doesn't look from here as though either of them will be amassing millions or collecting bonuses; but who knows? Perhaps bankers and corporation lawyers were dreamy and idealistic once upon a time.

One contemporary of mine, a bearded writer, gay and

successful, assured the company we were in the other day
that he felt no dissonance, indeed no sense of any difference
that mattered from friends who were younger than he is,
even from those who were much younger. Perhaps he has
made a decision to think that our differences from the young
need not be noticeable to the young if we ignore them ourselves. Then two distinguished old gentlemen were quizzed
on the radio recently about the words that are used to
describe the old – 'elderly', 'senior' and so on – and which
of them they preferred. Both of them dismissed the notion
that a special vocabulary of any sort was required to describe
people who have been alive for sixty years or more, so sure
were they both of their enduring energies and virtues, which
were neither impaired in any way nor significantly different
from those of much younger people. But I am always, and
often uncomfortably, aware of being an old person in the
eyes of the young, of my difference, of how the young may
think of me. If this is uncomfortable, it isn't painful; it is
simply a consequence of remembering how I thought of the
old when I was young. So sometimes, yes, I imagine horror,
ridicule, indifference; but I am also aware that the young are
likely to fear growing old themselves, and that they look
upon the old with awe as well as indifference, but also with
trepidation at the meaning of old age for them.

Auntie Annie was not my aunt at all, but the aunt of a friend
of my parents who taught the violin at the school I went to,
where my father taught the piano. Kit, the friend was called,
and Kit's Auntie Annie had been installed, eternally it

seemed to me, in a small upstairs room filled with an enormous feather bed, in which she lay back comfortably against her mountain of pillows. When I asked my mother why she stayed in bed all day, my mother told me – I was about eight at the time – that she was simply 'bedridden', a description I took to mean some kind of life choice, a desire for and pleasure in her bed. Everything in that room was feathery: the pillows and quilts, Auntie Annie's wild white hair and her colour-drained woollen bed jacket, the air in the room, all dust and feathers. Squeezed between the end of her bed and the wall was one of those enormous tallboys, with rows of tiny drawers as well as large ones and cupboards. The great thing about visiting Auntie Annie was that she would direct you firmly to one of that multitude of drawers in order to find something: a wine gum or a bull's-eye, a marble, a Kirby-grip, a tiny notebook, a doll's pencil. Sometimes these were presents intended for her visitors. Sometimes they were things she just wanted to show you. The treat was sitting on that billowing bed and following her detailed instructions.

I thought Auntie Annie must be the oldest person who had ever lived. Now I suspect that she was not much older than I am now. She also seemed the happiest person alive, as she laughed and smiled and pointed. I never saw her get out of bed, and no one I knew had ever seen her on her feet. There were even doubts that she had such things. I had double feelings about her. She seemed infinitely frail, almost transparent, a creature of all that dust and feathers. I knew that she must soon be going to die and that she was in some sense getting ready to do so. Yet I have always thought of her as living exactly as she wanted to, not exactly pampered, but indulged. I expect that was an illusion – perhaps she'd taken to her bed in mutiny – but it may be that that is how the young do sometimes think of the old, as strange and frail and at the end of their lives, but also as living life as they want to, fixed in their choices and their habits and attached even to their aches and pains, their complaints and their grumbling.

Yesterday evening, a freezing December evening, and unusually, I was walking up Bond Street from Piccadilly, making my way to the Private View of an old friend, a painter, now eighty, and as productive – no, more so – as he ever was in his youth. Everything in the street glittered. The expensive shops were closed, their gleaming windows full of garments cunningly constructed to look like armour, splints, slings, bandages: ideal for journalists reporting on the war in Afghanistan and hoping to be taken for combatants; less suited to those doomed to spending longish stretches of their declining years in hospital waiting-rooms. I worked in Bond Street years ago. Even then, it had glamour, though I thought it a seedy glamour, mothballed from the twenties and thirties and not for me. Expensive shops didn't direct their wares at the young in those days, and the few really grand shops in Bond Street were meant for middle-aged ladies; though there was Fenwicks, where I sometimes spent my lunch hour and don't remember buying anything much. It felt strange last night remembering myself more than fifty years ago. If I was transformed, barely the same person, the street had altered too. Money, display, elegance still, but it's fiercer now, in your face, no longer so seductively and silkily rich and classy, holding its own now through money (enormous quantities of it) even more than class. Money prevails now, money and shock and, perhaps, humour; though the jokes are ones I don't really get.

The office of the American weekly magazine where I worked was small and shabby. To reach it you went through a narrow door and passage and up some linoleum-covered stairs to two rooms above a dusty camera shop. One of the rooms of the office was filled with an enormous ticker-tape machine, beside which I sat. In the other room was my boss: a tiny, neat American, I remember, with a bow-tie, a moustache and a wife called Gloria who was about to have a baby. So was I, it turned out, though I hadn't known that when I was offered the job and accepted it. A moment of faintness and my tumbling admission meant that I was out on my ear by the following day. He'd been grooming me, he said, to interview MPs at the House of Commons. You couldn't send a pregnant woman to do that. There was no question in those days of women having or deserving it all, or even anything much, and I didn't complain.

When I think now about the relation of the old to the young and, somewhere within that, of the relation of the old to their young selves, I am grateful at least to be spared the particular pains of the goatish old man tortured by longing for a beautiful young woman, and ridiculous in his own eyes for being so: Chaucer's January and May, for instance, or Picasso, in that sequence of paintings of himself as an old Priapus and the girl with the ponytail. Yet that pain and its melancholy expression have also produced comedy and lyricism and a grim sort of wisdom about young women and their fathers. Think of Rochester's 'A Song of a Young Lady. To her Ancient Lover', for instance,

> Ancient Person, for whom I,
> All the flattering Youth defy;
> Long be it e're thou grow Old,
> Aking, shaking, Crazy Cold.
> But still continue as thou art,
> *Ancient Person of my Heart.*

I am reminded of an extraordinary sight from my youth. An icy-cold January morning more than fifty years ago, and I was walking my first son in his pram, trying to get him to sleep so that I could think my own thoughts for an hour or so. I remember walking to the round pond in Kensington Gardens and circling it to the east side, where I stopped to look back across the pond. A large man in a black coat stood on the edge of the water beside a woman, who was tall too, I remember, with what looked like golden hair in the winter sunlight. Suddenly, he turned and enveloped her in his coat and kissed her. I was intrigued and touched and hurried to the other side of the pond to get closer. There I recognised T. S. Eliot and his second wife, Valerie, whom he had married the year before. That marriage between a man of sixty-nine and a woman thirty-eight years younger than him seems to have been astonishingly happy.

Sexual relations between the old and the young are not always so easy, and J. M. Coetzee writes about difficult passions of that kind in several of his novels. In his *The Diary of a Bad Year*, for instance, an old South African writer now living in Australia is writing essays of opinion and reflection on the times: essays that are due to be prestigiously published as the fruit of a lifetime's wisdom and experience. The essays themselves sit on the top half of every page; and you can't help thinking of their presence in the novel as produced by an old man's economies or recycling habits, though they are also there to counter his more frantic imaginings with a decorous public voice. For sitting beneath them, on the bottom half of each page, are his dreamed-up moments of lust and longing and the possible sexual humiliation such feelings are likely to land him in.

He is instantly obsessed with Anya, the delectable young woman (she is partly Philippine, as if to alert us to the subservient part she is to play in his fantasy life) whom he meets on the first page of the novel in the laundry of the flats where they both live, she with her middle-aged lover. The writer is even more obsessed by what her thoughts and conversations with her lover may contain about him. He gives her a job as his typist and ostensible editor, though it is clear that she has no gift for either role. As his obsession broadens to include thoughts of her lover he imagines Anya's contempt for him and her lover's plans to defraud him, and takes his revenge by despising them both: she for her empty-headed beauty, her lover for dishonesty and a financier's philistinism. It is an ambiguous retaliation, however, since his targets are after all his own invention, and these imagined protagonists are set to evolve and complicate themselves far beyond his initial accounts of them.

The old writer expects to have his essays as summarily rejected by Anya as his desire would be, should he tell her of it. He imagines her complaining to her lover about his essays, describing his ideas as 'antiquated'. The essays must seem to her, he feels, 'like the bones of some odd extinct creature, half bird, half reptile, on the point of turning into stone'. He attributes to her his own sense of the depredations of age, though he wants to believe that he is different from most old people: 'I survey my elderly coevals and see all too many consumed with grouchiness, all too many who allow their helpless bafflement about the way things are going to turn into the main theme of their final years.' He finally settles for the possibility that Anya may secretly worry about him, may even protect him from her lover's plans to defraud him, that her feelings for him might after all be kindly ones, possessive and concerned. Perhaps she is saying to herself, 'I was the one he was in love with, in his old man's way, which I never minded as long as it did not go too far.'

A dread of youth's contempt for age, of young people's disgust at the weakness, ugliness, vulnerability of the old, struggles with the essayist's more measured and dignified sense of what as an old writer he wants – against the evidence – to believe is happening to him:

Growing detachment from the world is of course the experience of many writers as they grow older, grow cooler or colder. The texture of their prose becomes thinner, their treatment of character and action more schematic. The syndrome is usually ascribed to a waning of creative power; it is no doubt connected with the attenuation of physical powers, above all the power of desire.

The old must often fear the young: the exuberance of small children who head for your unsteady shins, the blithe indifference, impatience or even horror that the beautiful and the healthy may express towards the withered and infirm. Only now do I begin to realise that what I often thought of when I was young as the superiority of the old, their grand indifference to us, or even their manifest boredom with our tastes and passions, was perhaps something else entirely: a defence, a form of revenge and retaliation, or simply a proud refusal to expose oneself to scorn of any kind. I remember an ancient great-uncle and aunt, a pair of once red-headed sibling gnomes. My great-aunt pointed me out to her brother, as old people sweetly do at times point out the young to one another, with an 'Isn't she lovely?' asked fairly rhetorically. 'No!' he replied at once, without the slightest pause and not in the least rhetorically.

If I am spared the pains of the goat or the humiliations visited on the girlish, flirtatious old woman making, as they say, a fool of herself over a younger man, I am not spared the agonised love the old can feel for their grown-up children, a love just as susceptible to rejection and ridicule and fear in its own way as unrequited sexual desire. It is agonised, and hobbled, because it has always to be kept in check in the interests of the necessary development of their children's other potentially healthier and rival loves. There is, after all, a vast and menacing literature on the subject of clinging, pushing, overbearing and destructive parents. And the older they get the worse they can be. Turgenev's *Fathers and Sons* is rare for being intensely moving about the unrequited love harboured by the old for the young, especially of parents for their children. The novel begins with 'the uneasiness often felt by a young person who is no longer a child and who has returned to a place where people still see and think of them as a child.' The novel seems to be announcing its intention of presenting the case for the young and for their need to separate from their parents and their elders generally, to disown family and all determining ties and origins, or at least thoroughly to renegotiate relations with them. So our sympathy is immediately enlisted in favour of the young, until the moment when Arkady's father, still, in fact, only forty-four, overhears his son's friend, Barazov, talking of him as a 'retired man', who 'has had his day'. He feels foolish, out of it already. But more than that, he feels that he's losing his son and losing him to his clever young nihilist friend, and he wonders whether the young have 'something we don't have, some advantage over us. Youth? No! Not only youth. Could their advantage be that they have fewer upper-class traits and habits than we do?'

Class and politics often do feature in the conflict between

generations, though the conflict may more often arise when children wish to rise above their parents' class, above the class they themselves grew up in. At all events, class may figure as the clearest, most obvious and perhaps the most insurmountable face of family conflict between generations. And the old may come to represent some of the traditions and connections as well as the constraints and banalities of the past that need to be kicked away.

In fact, Arkady's father doesn't lose his son. Arkady returns after his student adventures and eventually marries and moves in with his father to run their estate. It is Bazarov's parents who lose their son so calamitously: first to his nihilism and the cynicism of his politics and the aridity of his sneering refusal of love, family, even feeling, and eventually to his careless death from typhoid. When he visits them at last, after three years of studying in St Petersburg, he not only brings his friend Arkady with him, he makes it plain that he finds his parents dull and simple-minded. Within three days he is off again, this son that his mother 'loved and feared beyond words', leaving his father bereft and miserably muttering to himself, 'he's bored with us now'. But before he and Arkady leave we watch the feast Bazarov's mother prepares for her prodigal son, and the hopeless array of emotions she so unnerves this son by expressing: 'Her eyes, fixed on Bazarov, expressed more than devotion and tenderness; there was sadness there, mixed with fear and curiosity, and a sort of meek reproach.'

Later, Bazarov returns for a few weeks, settling uncomfortably back into the family and helping his father with his primitive village doctoring. His parents tread on eggshells to avoid exasperating this extraordinary son of theirs, who has flown back into their lives and is to fly so swiftly out of them. His illness and death destroy them, though they live on, ancient, demented, visiting their son's grave together, where they are touchingly and compassionately watched as, side by side, 'they hung their poor heads like little lambs at noon'.

When our children are young we fear for them, are sometimes horizontal in our anxieties for them, though I also remember developing extra temporary skills and capacities to foresee disaster and even, for most of the time, to forestall it. One of my sons still managed to break his nose while he was reading and walking at the same time, and on another occasion fell headfirst down some steps on to a manhole cover and rose quite cheerfully to display the letter A neatly imprinted on his forehead. He will do such things again, and quite often does. But my fear never quite goes away, nor does the belief that it is my duty to protect my children from such mishaps, even when they live on the other side of the world. There were all those years when we taught ourselves to let our children take risks, move out of our sight and earshot, rehearse their independence, make their own choices and decisions. The fear didn't leave us, even when they travelled the world, married, had children, started jobs or gave them up. Even as our children overtake us mentally and physically, and in their experience and knowledge of the world, especially of the modern world they are so much better at than we are, we still fear for them. We suffer helplessly over their unhappiness, which we cannot begin to assuage or lessen, and for most of the time we are not even expected to sympathise or assist or take sides.

But then we also find that our perpetual fear for our children is accompanied by another fear, a fear *of* our children, of their speed and strength and certainties, of their differences from us, of their impatience at our inability to understand them or their lives. It is not that our children want us to become weak and die, but they want our dramas and our feelings to be contained, under control, manageable, secondary. We are no longer to be in the thick of it, no longer to think of ourselves as passionately engaged, and perhaps that is as it should be. In an earlier novel by Coetzee, *Elizabeth Costello*, a middle-aged son accompanies his famous old mother, a novelist, on a lecture tour, and endeavours to keep her in line as she threatens to outrage and quarrel with her audiences, shocking them with her sensitive person's ultra-liberal theories and arguments in ways that are unseemly to him. He can't bear her to get above herself, lose her self-protective instincts, embarrass him, enrage his wife, and so on. As he drives her to the airport after an especially provocative performance on her part, 'he pulls the car over, switches off the engine, takes his mother in his arms. He inhales the smell of cold cream, of old flesh. "There, there," he whispers in her ear. "There, there. It will soon be over."' And so it will.

8

Old Woman

Whew! What a relief to learn that the post-menopausal women of the Hadza hunter-gatherer people in Tanzania win prizes for their assiduous gathering of roots, honey and fruit! Apparently, conscientious grandmothers put in as much as seven hours a day, compared to teenagers and new brides with their paltry three hours, and married women with children, who do four and a half hours a day at most. Indeed, the fruits of foraging 'increased with age and experience, so that mature women achieved higher returns than teenagers, but, interestingly, the grandmothers' returns were still as high as those of women in their prime'.

I'm not sure that 'foraging' quite works as a metaphor for the range of duties expected of grandmothers in the Western world, but it's a good approximation. Presumably those busy Hadza grandmothers compensate for the bad hunting days endured by their husbands and sons and sons-in-law. In addition, their foraging enables them to provide the wherewithal for celebrating the return of their menfolk, with or without a booty of dead monkeys or squirrels. Jared Diamond, who reports on this research and its implications in his book *Why is Sex Fun?*, offers these old women's foraging skills as among a number of advantages human females gain for themselves – as well as conferring on society – by ceasing to be fertile long before they die, a combination which marks them off from almost all other female animals. Bernard Williams also congratulated women on their usefulness in old age. Once they are freed from child-bearing and the vicissitudes of sexual desirability (which do seem like vicissitudes from here, though they didn't always at the time), old women can serve the community in any number of ways. Since, by and large, women also live a good deal longer than men, some sort of explanation may be in order for this long period of infertile life enjoyed, if that is the word (and I think it may be), by women. Looking after their grandchildren and passing on aspects of their culture and history to the younger generation may be seen, from an evolutionary point of view, as a satisfactory trade-off for ceasing to produce children of their own. Indeed, it has always seemed pretty satisfactory to me, though clearly it doesn't seem so to some women, and especially not to those who for one reason or another have put off having children until their forties and may have come to regret doing so.

It is a relief to learn that we old women, disingenuously applauded for our 'change of life', are not just hanging about, consuming valuable resources and failing to pull our weight.

But reducing us to our natures, and then congratulating us on the perfect aptness of our biology, doesn't quite deal with the matter, and, besides, it's a tactic we're all too used to. Why are women so susceptible to biological generalisation? Why are our shared natural capacities and drawbacks triumphantly invoked in the teeth of extreme cultural variations among the ways societies mark and make use of women's biological differences from men? What sort of Darwinian explanation might be adduced to explain men's longer-lasting fertility and shorter lives? Or are those truths that are in no need of evolutionary or genetic explanation? Does the writing of books by philosophers or scientists or anthropologists – or even poets – about women's nature itself derive from men's role as hunters in earlier times? And though I like the idea that societies value old women for what they can tell the young about history and culture, the truth is that 'old wives' tales' have not been valued any more than 'old women' have been: 'old woman' is a term, after all, that may be used disparagingly about a human being of any age and either sex in a way that 'old man' can't and isn't, and 'old woman' used in that way certainly doesn't convey respect for the humanly robust or wise or even useful. There is the story of an old Irishwoman who was giving evidence before the eighteenth-century Scottish judge Lord Meadowbank and was being harassed by him to get on with it. She felt she should explain: 'Me Lord, I'm no schollard,' she said, 'but just an ould wife like yourself.'

Then women are usually found to be too young or too old for things that matter: they're too young for wisdom, and then suddenly they're too old for sex. There must surely be a few years when they're capable of both, perhaps even at the same time. In India women do most of the heavy carrying and lifting on building sites and on the land, because the men are needed for more skilled work; or, as one expert on these things insists, because the men are busy playing cards, drinking tea and solving the problems of the world. That particular division of labour reflects the still vastly unequal access of girls to education and training in India compared with boys. Yet nature is everywhere invoked to bolster and explain social and cultural habits as they affect women, so that women's physical weakness relative to men's will be respected when it comes in handy to do so, just as a female talent for sewing and cooking will be championed just so long as it remains firmly within the domestic and amateur spheres. Once money is to be made out of those activities, they become characteristically male ones, and women have to struggle just to join in. And what was my biology teacher at school up to when she told us that women should carry the suitcases rather than men because their larger hips made it easier for them to avoid clattering the suitcases against the calves of their legs?

Some time in the 1860s, before universal elementary education had been established in England, there were school inspectors who despaired of girls learning anything and remarked on what they thought of as innate incapacities when it came to reading and writing, let alone arithmetic: 'In some of the girls' schools very few of the children could write, and the writing was very bad . . . in several of the girls' schools the children do not learn arithmetic at all.' It was difficult to get some girls to go to school, and no bones were made about girls' inferior mental abilities; though one report contained the startling admission from a teacher that far more of the girls turned up for school when they had been assured that there would be no needlework (usually a matter of sewing shirts that the school sold for profit), but a real lesson, in which they might learn something. Perhaps not wasting time is a genetic inheritance for girls and women.

An additional irony was that at exactly the moment in the nineteenth century when despair about girls' intellectual capacities was most clamorously voiced, a new need for a great number of teachers meant that a vast army of girls and young women was hurriedly recruited and perfunctorily trained to teach the next generation of children. But that was all right too. They were paid very little and their natural intellectual inferiority may be said to have set in train a century and a half of disparagement of the teaching profession, almost certainly on the grounds that a majority of teachers were then, and have always been, women. That long history of disparagement has offered comfort to millions of parents and Secretaries of State for Education and is currently heard again in order to explain the relative failure of boys at school and the urgent need for teachers to take an MOT test every five years and to abide by an official Code of Conduct during holidays as well as term time.

*

There should be a special word to describe the sometimes unusual course of women's lives; unusual, that is, compared with the lives of the men they live among. It would need to be a positive word that discourages penalties for what may be thought of as the wavering or erratic movements of women's working lives, and for the periods when they may need to concentrate on producing or bringing up children or caring for older relations. I rather like 'saccadic'. Old age might then be thought of as a time when women catch up on interests and occupations they had no time for when they were younger. Their life trajectories are, at the very least, able to demonstrate how time may be differently used and valued, so that the years after sixty (and more women than men can look forward to those years) might no longer be thought of as a tapering-off or summing-up, or as an over-ture to the end, but as a time for experiment, change, novelty – and just as much for men as for women. Yet for a long time, women have been expected to retire from work earlier than men, for reasons which must have more to do with controlling employment than with men's and women's abilities to do productive work in their old age.

You could say that if women are fertile only between the ages of roughly thirteen and forty-five and then only inter-mittently, and if men are capable of impregnating women ceaselessly from about fourteen to ninety, there is likely to be conflict and some inequality of access to women, a dis-parity which all societies organise against in some way or other: polygamy, serial monogamy with younger and younger women, enforced female chastity, and so on. Earlier

male deaths could even count as one strategy for dealing
with the problem. In Western societies the conflict takes an
economic form as a rule and is focused on paid work and on
the bringing-up of children, which is still seen as the respon-
sibility of women, despite the greater involvement of men
these days. It is, for instance, still usual for the woman in a
family to organise what it is that the man should do as his
share. Apparently inflexible beliefs about the differences
between men and women are usually modified or even abandoned as soon as there is a crisis or if men are for some
reason reluctant to perform certain tasks. So law, medicine,
teaching, preaching, the Civil Service have all changed their
gender requirements as soon as there has been a need for
more entrants; though no society that I know of has solved
the problem for women of doing work as it is organised for
men to do it while bringing up children at the same time.

For some years after I was ejected from the Bond Street
office of that American weekly magazine, I worked as a
reader and editor for a publisher. I thought myself lucky to
find such work and even lucky to be paid £7 10s for the
three days a week that I went into the office to do it, more
than half of which I handed over to a charming eighty-year-
old Welsh woman, once a nurse (a generic grandmother
herself, though she had never had children of her own), for
looking after my son, and then another son. Editing was the
kind of work graduate women of my generation in the
1950s, particularly ones who were about to have babies or
had had them already, were grateful for. It led nowhere, but
it had the advantage of not being housework while allowing

us to step out of the confinement of our flats and houses, and it demanded little commitment from us. Our gratitude was almost enough. We hoped that our husbands would earn just about what was needed to keep us and any children we might have, while, more importantly, embarking on and furthering something that might be called a career.

There were other advantages to the work I did. I learned to type quite fast without looking at my hands and to write pithy reports about what I thought was good or bad about the books I was reading, something I had by no means learned to do at university, where I was mainly engaged in writing what I hoped my tutors wanted to read (and most of the time didn't want to read, because, inevitably, they already knew far more about the subject than I did). I knew very few women of my age then who thought about careers: that is, about work that would develop and perhaps continue to absorb them to the ends of their lives. Many of them worked rather as I did, casually, part-time, on the fringes. Some of them took up crafts: pottery, interior decoration, patchwork quilts, making jewellery, cooking. A few of my generation of women did go into medicine, the law, the Civil Service, journalism, even the theatre; and among the quite large number of my women friends who did not go to university (there were still rather few university places for women in the 1950s, after all), several became writers.

I had no wish to become a proper publisher, and in those days I'd have had a pretty slim chance of becoming one even if I had wanted to. Yet many of my contemporaries somehow fell into careers in the end, as I did, without quite realising we were doing so. Some of us became tired of our genteel foraging in publishers' offices or with writing anonymous book reviews for *The Times Literary Supplement*. But it took some time for me to realise that the working part of my life that took me out of the house had a certain pointlessness to it.

Then, when my older son and his friends were eleven and about to go to secondary school, many of them were turned down by the schools of their and our choice, just as many children are today, though the schools in question were not selective schools but popular ones. For a mad moment I imagined starting a school for these rejected children and inviting my friends to teach them. But I knew nothing about teaching and nor did they, nor was I planning to charge fees or pay the teachers. So most of us put up with the schools our children were sent to, and I decided to try my hand at teaching, and became an English teacher in a large London comprehensive, the very one that had turned my son down, as it happens; and not long afterwards, he joined me at that school. I was too old at thirty-six to be trained at state expense, I was told, so I learned on the job as best I could, and it wasn't easy. But I suppose that after about three years I had learned how to teach, more or less, and I found myself enjoying the children I taught, the classrooms I taught them in, English teaching.

In fact, I became passionately interested in teaching, and particularly in teaching English. It was not just that I enjoyed doing it. I found the whole business of learning how to teach, and of children learning how to learn, more interesting than anything I had ever done before. I had never imagined being as absorbed by anything as I was then. I read everything I could find on the subject. My children used to tease me as I lay in the garden in the holidays reading books with titles that might begin with the word 'Towards' or 'Beyond' , followed by a trio of extremely abstract nouns. They hoped that one day I might be found reading a book whose title contained words like 'Now' and even 'Then'. Several years later I was actually paid to follow a full-time course on language at London University (something that would be unheard of nowadays). From there I went on to teach at that university and to train English teachers and supervise their higher degrees and research. I spent the last twenty-two years of my working life teaching graduate English teachers, and bizarrely and belatedly in possession at last of what might be accounted a 'career'.

I offer this history because in some ways it matches the development of their work in the lives of many middle-class women graduates of my age; but it is necessary to stress that that particular drift towards a career was probably an almost exclusively middle-class story and characteristic of the 1950s. There was often a desultory and uncertain beginning, work that could be fitted round children and school holidays. Yet my husband, my parents, most of the adults with whom I grew up, expected me to work, to be able to earn my living, and even to do something that I would find interesting. My father's unmarried aunts had all taught in schools or worked as civil servants. My mother painted or drew every day of her life. But there was no encouragement

to be ambitious, to think about the future or about the kind
of life you might want to live later, when your children had
left home. Ambition was discouraged in women; indeed, an
ambitious woman attracted opprobrium to herself, and perhaps that was why I avoided it, though I think I was also
afraid of failure, of looking silly. I enjoyed my part-time
jobs, being with my children for some of the time, but not
all of the time. So for many of us, picking up relatively badly
paid, disregarded work that was vaguely literary or tenu-
ously appropriate to whatever we'd studied at university
was about all we hoped for. It had the advantage of being
quite difficult to fail at.

I have become a grandmother in a very different world. It is
a world where some of us may eventually have gathered
careers for ourselves, and where we expect our daughters as
well as our sons to have them too. Not untypically, none of
my three children has a conventionally full-time job, though
they could all be said to have careers and to work a good deal
of the time. Our grandmotherly expertise is no longer con-
fined to sucking eggs, and there is a high probability that we
will outlive our male partners. The erratic relation we have
had to paid work during the course of our lives may well
stand us in good stead now in retirement. We expect to be
paid for some of what we do, but by no means for everything. Many of us work quite hard at something or other that
is unpaid.

Some of the old men I know are uncomfortably cast
adrift by their loss of power, of work, of purpose, of

routine, of money, and of somewhere that is not home to go to. They don't necessarily feel in their sixties and seventies like those government ministers it's difficult to believe, who claim to retire from office in order 'to spend more time with their families'. It may have been easier for the women I know to cope with their new status in retirement. It feels familiar. Even at my most professional I felt like an amateur. I was used to working at the kitchen table, marking, making classroom materials, writing shopping lists in meetings or while waiting to teach a class or a seminar or give a lecture, fitting parents' evenings and morning assemblies into slots snatched from demanding schedules. I remained ignorant and innocent of what makes institutions function so badly, and continued until the end – despite the evidence – to believe that committee meetings were meant for discussing items on the agenda, not for rubber-stamping what had in fact been decided elsewhere beforehand. My working life was always conducted in tandem with being a mother. And I was a daughter during that time too, and then a grand-mother during the final years of it. I used to get to my office very early and I almost never had lunch. I smoked instead. Now I relish later mornings and proper lunches and I don't smoke any more. Family relations have always been cen-trally important to women like me throughout our lives, and it was always up to us to work out how to combine family and work. The main discovery I've made in retire-ment is friends. Friendship withered while I worked. Now it flourishes.

There is an article in the newspaper today announcing that

women in their late twenties or early thirties – Thatcher children, it calls them – are so 'self-assured' that they now want to put family before career simply because they feel able to demand working conditions that suit them. The implication is that ambition and success need not rule out having children and a properly attended-to sexual partnership, since clever young women are nowadays in a position to negotiate for what suits them as mothers and wives. If this is true, hurrah! It is impossible not to wonder, however, whether such confidence will survive the present economic downturn. And for the majority of working women, often part-time and paid the minimum wage, such possibilities remain a dream. There is something dispiriting about television programmes and newspaper articles that offer a version of feminism in which talk of 'glass ceilings' and 'having it all' makes the appalling employment possibilities for the majority of women – and a very large number of men too – seem beside the point. As though, through a version of the 'trickle-down effect', all women will somehow gain if there are a few more women bankers receiving monstrous bonuses, a few more television presenters on absurdly high salaries. It is hard enough to see quite how most women could possibly have benefited from having a woman as Prime Minister or Foreign Secretary or Home Secretary, though I suppose there are girls growing up now who experience no brake on their ambition and no limit to the scope of what they could try for. And that is a good thing, if hardly revolutionary.

*

We should no doubt thank our stars for what can seem rather patronising reassurances that old women have their uses, for there are still societies where that is by no means a certainty, where fates not so different from sati (when Hindu widows, who might, in fact, be very young, were expected to immolate themselves on their dead husbands' pyres) are common. Old women have not always been thought of benignly as either useful or harmless. In fact, there is a long tradition of grossly denatured and hideous old women, in legend and in literature, whose terrifying ugliness may be witch-like, wicked, possessed of some magical and demonic strength. There is that scene in Pushkin's *The Queen of Spades*, where the old countess, divested of the much mocked excesses of her dress and wig and elaborate headdress, is glimpsed as she really is – bald, swollen, flabby – while 'the rocking movements of the horrible old woman seemed to be produced not by her but by some hidden galvanic power'. There is the crazed malevolence of Mrs Sinclair, the brothel-keeper in Samuel Richardson's *Clarissa*, an archetypally monstrous figure, a woman gone spectacularly wrong and beyond anything that is humanly recognisable. The threat of madness, of hysteria, of forms of unspeakable physical decay and disease, is manifested in such women as the collapse and deterioration of body and face, deformities which may be read off as the expression of a terrible moral turpitude, worse than the most tyrannical brutality precisely because it exists eerily and unnaturally in a woman. Richardson is almost babbling and dribbling with the sheer excessiveness of what he has to tell us about Mrs Sinclair:

The old dragon straddled up to her, with her arms kemboed again – her eyebrows erect, like the bristles upon a hog's back and, scowling over her shortened nose, more than half-hid her ferret eyes. Her mouth was distorted. She pouted out her blubber-lips, as if to bellows up wind and sputter into her horse-nostrils; and her chin was curdled, and more than usually prominent with passion.

Ideally, female beauty should modulate into inoffensive invisibility. According to the alternative account, the erosion of beauty and of all that is understood as essentially feminine leaves a woman's soul – inclined to emptiness in the first place, after all – peculiarly vulnerable to iniquity. It is a thoroughly sorry tale.

The American poet Frederick Seidel recently published a poem called 'Climbing Everest', in which an old man has breathless sex with a young woman, risky for both of them. It is a brilliant and funny poem, which acts out the exhilaration and the humiliating struggle of it all and compares the sexual adventure to climbing Everest and waking up ignominiously in an oxygen tent, presumably at base camp. Seidel received some hostile correspondence when it was published in America, directed particularly at the poem's last verse:

A naked woman my age is just a total nightmare,
But right now one is coming through the door
With a mop, to mop up the cow flops on the floor.
She kisses the train wreck in the tent and combs his white
    hair.

I find I am more moved by the lines than offended. The old woman's body may be 'just a total nightmare', but the nightmare is the man's nightmare, the product of his impossible desire for youth, of his own physical disintegration, even his dependence on the old woman's kindness and practicality. It is his nightmare, not hers. There can't be many women of my age (which is older still than Seidel's) who get pleasure from looking at their own bodies or inhabiting them. But we have grown used to them. They don't arouse the desire of old men or, indeed, of young men, but they don't give us nightmares, and we may be luckier than the poem's old man in that for most of the time we manage to get our bodies to do the things we want them to do: possible things, that is, like cleaning up messes, kissing the heads of our poor deluded partners and even climbing miniature Everests of our own. It is true, however, that our Donor Cards, offering our organs to some unfortunate, are likely to be found redundant by now. My Great-Aunt Clara offered her body to University College Hospital, but when she died at eighty-eight they turned it down.

Picasso once announced that, 'like every artist, I am first of all a painter of women'. I don't think he meant old women, though there are wonderful paintings of old women by Giorgione and Velázquez and Lucian Freud, for instance, all of them fully dressed, as far as I can remember. How are women to come to terms with the kind of male adoration of female beauty so many painters have gone in for? We can adore it too, I suppose, and women often do enjoy the

beauty of other women; or we can view it with the kind of
irony Charlotte Brontë gets Lucy to express in *Villette* as she
gazes at the gloriously overblown *Cleopatra* in Villette's
National Gallery, ridiculing its excesses while also marvelling at the power emanating from this woman, whose image
is so much more seductive, after all, than the dreary and
diminutive quartet of pictures entitled *La vie d'une femme* that
the *Cleopatra* so richly outclasses. It is not only that we are
turned into generic 'woman' by such visions and required to
share a man's account of them in a sporting spirit: it is that
most of us are also bound to fail the test set by what such
women can, rarely and remarkably, manage to be.

It is nearly fifty years since I translated the memoir written by Fernande Olivier, Picasso's first known love and
model. She wrote *Picasso and His Friends* many years after she
had parted from the painter, when she must have been well
into her fifties. Rereading my translation, I am embarrassed
to remember some of the difficulties I had turning her
direct, childlike and also amusing French into an equivalent
English, and I'm not sure that I succeeded. I was in awe both
of her legendary beauty and of the fact that as a writer she
was much older than I was, indeed older than my mother.
But I think I also slightly despised her for being a beauty at
all, for living off her beauty, as it seemed to me then. I used
a voice for hers that was a bit like my mother's: old-fashioned
schoolgirl, I thought of it. My mother had been a student at
the Slade in the late 1920s and rather a beauty herself, and
she would have been living in Paris when Fernande was
remembering her youth and writing about it. The difficulties

of translation were compounded by my ambivalence about the strong and beautiful young woman Fernande must have been, and by my sense that the book was written out of a complicated anger at the loss of her beauty and at the possibility that that beauty had been her sole ticket to the glamorous world she inhabited with Picasso between 1903 and 1912. 'I spent the most precious years of my life with Picasso,' she wrote, 'the years when I was happiest. The end of that era saw the end of most of my youth and all my illusions.' The book begins with her remembering herself in the early days:

> When I first made my appearance in that world I was young, rather timid, enthusiastic and extremely proud. There is a tendency in France, particularly among intellectuals, to regard women as incapable of serious thought. I sensed this, and it paralysed me. So I contented myself with listening. I believed in the profundity of the ideas I heard exchanged. I listened, passionately attentive, but I never dared utter an opinion of my own. I only joined in the conversation when 'my great artists' relaxed and started enjoying themselves like children. Only then had I the courage to shine and be myself, and if I did shine it was not just physically. I had a reputation for being witty at times and even satirical, though I hope I was kind and fair as well.

Fernande Olivier became an artist, affected by Picasso's work, yet with a fluency and flair of her own. I am reminded again of Lucy in *Villette* working out how as a young woman she could be simultaneously clever, creative and loved by a man, here her employer and teacher, Paul.

> A 'woman of intellect,' it appeared, was a sort of *lusus naturæ,* a luckless accident, a thing for which there was neither place nor use in creation, wanted neither as wife nor worker. Beauty anticipated her in the first office. He believed in his soul that lovely, placid, and passive mediocrity was the only pillow on which manly thought and sense could find rest for its aching temples.

Fernande Olivier was a tall, intelligent young woman, and Picasso often represented her as grandly monumental. She was by no means placid or passive. Picasso used her as a model and, you might say, as an inspiration, for his paintings and sculptures, during one of the most productive periods of his life, until he finally exchanged her for another beautiful young woman, and then another and another. Fernande Olivier remembers the family she emerged from:

> I still remember how my parents, who were small-scale manufacturers of artificial flowers, feathers and potted shrubs, much preferred the stiff, shiny plants produced in their workshops to real plants, whose only purpose in their eyes was to serve as models for their copies.

The ironies are multiple, and Fernande recognised them, so that her book is both a recreation of the world of her youth and its inhabitants, and also a subtle reflection on it and on the extraordinary art that was produced around her and that she participated in. She is simultaneously sour and philosophical. She knew that there would always be many young women jostling for the position she occupied, and that those who were chosen felt flattered, proud, remarkable. Yet almost all of them suffered as Fernande did when they were abandoned: 'I know some of the women who lived with those artists, companions of the good and the bad hours of their youth: and they are growing old alone too, with only their memories as constant companions.' I felt lucky as I read and translated that book. At least, no one would ever say of me: 'She was once a beauty, you know.'

I remember occasionally snorting with rage at Lord Clark's television series *Civilisation*, in 1969, with its reduction of women to models for madonnas, simultaneously sexy and angelic, as it seemed to me, rather than potential participants of any kind in what might be thought of as civilisation; and then later jibbing at John Berger's insistence, in his *Ways of Seeing*, that

Men look at women. Women watch themselves being looked at. This determines not only most relations between men and women but also the relation of women to themselves. The surveyor of woman in herself is male: the surveyed female. Thus she turns herself into an object – and most particularly an object of vision: a sight.

I also recognised a good deal of truth in what he was saying, though I have always felt uncertain about the character and the extent of women's complicity in such transactions. Is it complicity or narcissism, or is it some idea of ourselves that was born and might thrive independently of men's interest in us? Most women would say, I think, that they care at least as much about how other women view them as about how men do.

I have been looking at photographs of myself with some of my friends when we were young (I shall return to them later), and we seem in them – as I suppose many groups of young women still are – hopelessly self-conscious, beadily aware of ourselves and each other as objects of attention, including our own. I remember that in my twenties I confessed to a philosopher friend of mine that I wasn't sure whether I would be able to recognise myself without the assistance of another person's view of me. He seemed shocked to hear such a thing, as if I should have been able to construct and possess a personality and an appearance for myself without extraneous clues as to how to do it; as he, I assumed, felt able to. I don't think I envied my best friend at school and at university, who was a beauty. The love and desire and sheer interest she inspired seemed at times to clip her wings, diminish her freedom, set her apart from the rest of us. I felt that it was even harder for her than it was for me to disentangle herself from men's thoughts and feelings about us, and harder to know what she thought of the men themselves. And even then there was something sad about the dazzling beauty of the few. It seemed always to announce its own deliquescence, tragedy, loss. For the rest of us there was simply change to worry about, and change might even turn out to be intriguing, an improvement, as I think it has been for many women.

I have not much first-hand experience of uselessness or monstrousness, nor any sense that I might be looked at with pity, as someone who must once have been beautiful and is so no longer. Instead, I bask in a new invisibility, which allows me to walk the streets and gaze at the world without attracting the least attention. And there is pleasure to be had from that. I sit on the tops of buses with my Freedom Pass and gaze into the windows above the shops. I listen in to conversations, wonder at the possible lives of my fellow passengers, marvel at the idiocies encouraged by mobile phones, measure the progress of the seasons by examining the trees. And no one cares. There was a time when such naked curiosity would have provoked a 'Who do you think *you're* looking at?' or 'Penny for them' or even 'It may never happen.' But no longer. Old age confers a delicious privacy in public places. There is something absurd, I suppose, in the thought that only in old age may women sit comfortably alone among people they don't know, happily ignored, unwatched and free, though I have to confess that I still hate sitting alone in cafés or restaurants, as I know a younger generation of women likes to do.

Simone de Beauvoir had no doubt that women are liberated by old age as men are not:

For women in particular the last age represents liberation: under their husbands' thumbs all their lives and
occupied with caring for their children, they can at last
think about themselves. Middle-class Japanese women,
who are kept under tight control, often enjoy a lively old
age. I have been told of some who have got divorced at 70
in order to make the most of their last years, and who are
endlessly grateful.

There is something essential missing from that, and perhaps I am in danger of missing it too. De Beauvoir is
certainly not writing from personal experience, and women
divorce their husbands at all ages nowadays, after all, and
don't need to wait until their seventies, even in Japan. I
don't think Simone de Beauvoir ever lived with anyone,
even Sartre, for long, if at all, and she seems not to have
known that there are pleasures as well as trials in living with
someone else, as I have done for fifty-four years. I have to
admit that if I glory in my invisibility, it is within the safety
of a constant companionship as well as friendships of all
kinds. Neither de Beauvoir nor I can be saying, surely, either
that solitude, loneliness, are what old age peculiarly and
delightfully offers or that such states are commonly desired
by women of any age. Women who have lived with someone else all their lives, whether as wives or companions or
mothers, are unlikely to find it easy to live alone, in old age
or earlier, though many learn to do so when they have to,
and they may, I am sure, feel freed in some ways, just as de
Beauvoir hopes they will. But, for many women, their

duties as carers hardly cease with age; indeed, they often increase.

I have had women friends who have spent most of their lives alone, and others who have had to live alone during the last years of their lives. By and large they have all done well, better than many men who are left to live on their own. But de Beauvoir strikes a rare false note for me here, produced, I dare say, by her inveterate desire to spring women from their marriage traps. Perhaps there really are Japanese women delightedly divorcing their husbands in their seventies, but I shall not emulate them. The women who enjoy their solitude in old age, and there are many such women, have had time to get used to it. For those who come late to solitude there must be a lot of pain and a great deal to learn.

9

Late

Edward Said had been ill with chronic leukaemia for twelve years when he died at the age of sixty-seven in 2003. He was characteristically productive throughout those years, and some of the last of his writings are to be found in a book called *On Late Style*. It is a book of essays assembled posthumously by his wife Mariam and his friend Michael Wood and it starts from a passionate reading of the egregiously difficult Theodor Adorno's work on what he termed *Spätstil*: difficulty being, both for Adorno and for Said, an aspect of late style itself.

The book is partly inspired by Said's interest in Adorno's proposition that some artists produce their most powerful and original work at the end of their lives. Adorno developed his idea of late style to explain Beethoven's extraordinary late quartets; and Said starts from there too, before moving on to the work of other composers and musicians, particularly Richard Strauss and Glenn Gould. He also wants to consider the idea's importance for the ageing Adorno himself, with its claim to the possibility of a new kind of energy and brilliance in old age:

> Lateness is being at the end, fully conscious, full of memory, and also very (even preternaturally) aware of the present. Adorno, like Beethoven, becomes therefore a figure of lateness itself, an untimely, scandalous, even catastrophic commentator on the present.

So lateness becomes something more than a ripe old age within Said's account of it. Even the tensions and contradictions of the mature young Mozart's *Così fan tutte* qualify the opera, in Said's eyes, to be thought of as meeting Adorno's requirements for late style. For this notion of lateness is stretched, it seems, to include absence, banishment, denial; and Said appears to allow *Così fan tutte* into the fold because of the harshness of the world that Mozart so brilliantly keeps out of the music: 'But we should not, I think, believe that the candid fun of the work does any more than hold its ominous vision in abeyance'.

Said is determinedly not interested in the possibility of an 'unearthly serenity' possessed (or looked for) in occasional late works of art, among which he includes *The Tempest* and *The Winter's Tale*, as plays which deliver themselves finally from dissonance and conflict to 'harmony and resolution'. Instead, he looks for 'intransigence, difficulty and unresolved contradiction' as characteristic strengths of the late works he has in mind. What if, he asks, age and ill

health and the prospect of death don't produce the serenity of 'ripeness is all'? What if, instead, some artists are
released into a new transgressiveness and defiance, which
make possible the enacting and the recognition of an
'anachronistic heroism', perhaps a new freedom? What
might we take from Adorno's description of Beethoven in
the late works 'as a lamenting personality', and from the
works themselves, in Said's words, as full of 'unsynthesised
fragmentariness' (a state of affairs, I presume, just this side
of total distintegration), evidence of a lifetime's absorption
and creative use of the rules, followed by a furious upsetting of them?

Said takes Adorno's lateness to mean most of the things
the word can mean in English. There are echoes of 'late' as
in dead or in the past, but there is also 'late' in the sense of
'after', of not being there for what's happening now, of
missing something, not in or on time, or even 'late' as in
the case of Adorno himself, 'because so much of what he
does militated ferociously against his own time' while, as
Said puts it, also being 'preternaturally aware of the present'. This last 'late' corresponds for Said to untimeliness,
being out of one's own times, not belonging, displaced and
even exiled from the contemporary world that is still the
world you inhabit. For an artist like Beethoven that meant
being devastatingly ahead of his contemporaries, beyond
them, beyond their understanding or experience, as his late
quartets and other work must indeed have been for composers and musicians of the day, and especially for his
audiences.

Said ends with an affirmation, inspired by reading the
poems of the Greek poet Cavafy, all of which were published
posthumously (another meaning for 'late'). Such writing
may express

> disenchantment and pleasure without resolving the
> contradiction between them. What holds them in ten-
> sion . . . is the artist's mature subjectivity, stripped of
> hubris and pomposity, unashamed either of its fallibility
> or of the modest assurance it has gained as a result of age
> and exile.

So lateness, old age, could allow for confidence, simplicity, wisdom, without the effort and the showiness that may
go with youthful ambition. It could mean not caring what
other people think, not needing acclaim, success, reassurance. Said's book has admirable energy and optimism. It is
surely impressive to think of him teaching and writing in this
way and on this subject when he was mortally ill and knew
that he hadn't long to live. He writes as well as, if not better
than, he ever has about particular works of art. For instance,
he has Proust and Lampedusa at the end of their lives sharing an ability to depict 'an immobilized present animated and
enlarged by a sustained reflection on the past'.

John Updike's last novels concentrated on the lives of old
writers and painters, but in an article he wrote a year or two
before he died about the artistic productions of the old he is
wanly sceptical of Said's claims, examining them in the light

of Shakespeare's last plays and quoting with approval Eve Kosofsky Sedgwick's less than ecstatic take on the late-flowering epiphany postulated by Said. All 'late style' amounts to, Updike suggests, are some more or less

> intelligible performances by old brilliant people, whether artists, scientists, or intellectuals, where the bare outlines of a creative idiom seem finally to emerge from what had been the obscuring puppy fat of personableness, timeliness, or sometimes even of coherent sense.

Updike was happy quoting someone else's 'senile sublime' as a more probable genre for work by old writers, but worried that late works were more likely to be characterised by what he called 'a translucent thinness' than by the roaring of outraged and outrageous old lions. His was an altogether more melancholy, less exalted, view of late work, and particularly of late writing. 'What does haunt late works is the author's previous works: he is burdensomely conscious that he has been cast, unlike his ingénu self, as an author who writes in a certain way, with the inexorable consistency of his own handwriting.' Martin Amis, sadly and exuberantly, read Updike's final book of stories (posthumously published) as mostly 'products of nothing more than professional habit', written with a late tin ear. Updike might have acknowledged the recycling, and the diagnosis and its cause, though hardly with delight, I imagine. Even Iris Murdoch's last novel, *Jackson's Dilemma*, the one she didn't remember writing by the time she was sent its proofs to correct, did not present, for Updike, 'a steep falling-off. It has wispy, stylized, and casually irrational elements, but so do her major works.' There was bound to be 'a geriatric ebb of energy', he insisted, so that the 'premature embrace of silence' in a writer like Henry Green had 'a kind of gallantry, a Rimbaudesque flamboyance' to it.

Said refused to give up on the big league of great artists and refused to admit to weakness, failure, deterioration, for himself or for his musical and literary heroes. Updike was interested in what happens when you do admit to the effects of age, to the withering of promise and the reduction of energy. That is moving too. Not all Said's excavations of lateness are, in fact, triumphalist. Lament, nostalgia, even paralysis are invoked too. Nor did he generalise from his exceptional artists to the rest of us. But the attraction of lateness for Said, connecting him as it did with the themes of his early work, was this idea of 'untimeliness': being left behind and out of step with the times, on the one hand, while managing to be simultaneously ahead of the times on the other; and it does have some of the beauties and advantages he claimed for it. It is felt as a sort of exile, giving edge and distance to an outsider's or exile's focus on the times. The idea clearly resonated for Said with a lifetime of belonging to more than one culture and of exploiting his particular experience of rootedness and its opposite in his scholarly and critical work and in his political advocacy on behalf of Palestine. The memoir he wrote in the late 1990s, when he was already ill, was called *Out of Place*.

*

Trying once to understand why my father had always seemed to me an outsider and a tragic figure, who in many ways was neither, I once wrote of him:

> My father spent most of his life among women . . . but I think he was most at ease, not among men, but in the romantic and idealised male company his reading offered him: European, mostly nineteenth-century, fenced off from the local and domestic English world of his own life, from the female, the family, the modern and even, perhaps, from the American.

He was a musician, a teacher, a solitary reader of literature in five or six languages. He had also been a precocious boy, as Said and his heroes must have been too: musically and linguistically gifted, miraculously full of promise. My memories of my father in middle and old age include the sense of that promise, of its having once been there and left its traces, though its flowering had been before my time. I think I may even have grown up wondering whether my arrival in the world hadn't dangerously coincided with the moment when the promise may suddenly have lapsed: for as far back as I can remember, that promise and talent had stiffened to dryness, oddness, eccentricity, even some loss of confidence as a pianist, despite the survival of a brittle authority over his own well-guarded areas of knowledge.

Perhaps the tragedy is my tragedy, and the lateness my lateness as well as his, because I came too late to witness his promise and bask in it. I took it on trust, knew that I would never measure up to it, felt it as something almost tangible that had, nonetheless, been carelessly blown away. I accepted his retreat into a past that was not quite his own past, not *his* childhood or youth. It was a past he'd found for himself in his reading and in late nineteenth-century and early twentieth-century 'modern' music: literature and music that could stand their ground against the contempt and neglect of the world he lived in now. He found it easier in old age to bear the challenge of the really young than the achievement of his contemporaries. His most successful contemporaries could be thought of as having come to terms with prevailing standards and demands, perhaps meretriciously. They had been received into that suspect world, were in one or two cases even revered by it. Retreat from that world must have seemed to my father to be the only decent response. The incomprehensible preferences of his children and grandchildren were comparatively easy to endure.

The critic Robert Storr has written about the extremely late work of the sculptor Louise Bourgeois (she is at least ninety-eight), and he starts from the nonsense humming and singing she goes in for nowadays as she works, what he calls 'a coded lullaby', indecipherable to others, as if she has outlived herself and us and is singing to some still unborn listeners. She has, however, retained her sharp mind and tongue and a ferocious temper. Her continuous narratives and commentary, both spoken and written, have finally stopped, but the work and the singing haven't. Storr compares her with her near-contemporary, Willem de Kooning, who was diagnosed with Alzheimer's in his seventies, yet continued to paint 'inventively and with astonishing virtuosity' for nearly ten years until stopping completely some years before his death at ninety-three. Storr explains de Kooning's continued productivity as the result of an almost 'uncanny ability to tap into and rejuvenate the roots of the classical tradition that passed through his consciousness and his body like veins and arteries after decades of tinkering with studio recipes and choreographing his motions in relation to the canvas.'

Storr is not suggesting that Bourgeois is suffering from dementia, though he does assume that aspects of her memory have deserted her, and that as a result her recent work is marked not so much by Updike's dreaded repetitiveness as by a process of abstraction which makes use of what for her is by now tried and tested and ready-made and which relies on memory to be so. Yet Bourgeois has always been contradictory about her reliance on memory. She has often announced that 'everything I do was inspired by my early life', but she has also explained, as she did in an interview in 1990, 'When I went back to France two or three years ago, I discovered that it is impossible for me to work because the past comes back, and my energy is spent in remembering, instead of working. Instead of making new things, I mope about the past.' Both things were true and they still are. But the distillation of those memories may now exist for her in the forms she has over many years bestowed on them, and it is those forms that continue to beget new ones rather than the memories themselves. So Storr sees this as a process of abstraction and as continuous with her earlier work, but as more in evidence now than in the past, not least because the storytelling in her art and in her writing may still go on, but it is silent now. Bourgeois's recent, late works have taught him, and others who write about her, something vital about her early work as well. Turning from these late works to her earlier ones, Storr has discovered, he writes, 'how their mesmerising textuality has distracted people from, and in some cases blinded them to, the manifest physical and perceptual realities of Bourgeois's art, and in particular its essential, protean abstractness.'

Linda Nochlin, the American art critic and historian, rejects any categorising of Bourgeois's late work as either elegiac or as making 'a dissonant break' with her earlier work. Rather, she sees the late work as continuous in many ways with what went before, but as about old age itself, a response to the artist's current situation, actually embodying and describing the realities of ageing and disintegration, but in two different ways. What Nochlin calls her 'soft' work, the stuffed and stitched figures, often roughly and crudely put together, add up to objectified accounts of the 'aging body itself, the prey of gravity', vulnerable, sagging, bulky, absurd – though they are also affectionately and delightedly placed in encouraging sexual proximity to one another. The discarded, cast-off clothing, the limply waiting, hanging garments, silky and delicate, collectively constitute 'a memorial to Bourgeois's own lost, youthful, sexy body' and invoke in their unworn emptiness 'the pre-monition of dying'.

Meanwhile, what Nochlin calls the 'hard' work, especially her silver model of the Institute of Fine Arts in New York, stands in for Nochlin (who was a student there and has then spent a lifetime teaching and researching in the same place) as the other aspect of her own and perhaps Bourgeois's struggle, understood at last, though not resolved, in old age: the demands of work, of 'scholarship, rigour, discipline, the realm of reason', a world that Nochlin (if not Bourgeois) associates with men; a world which resists the lumpy, squirming bodily pleasures apparently enjoyed by some of Bourgeois's stitched and stuffed creations.

It is as well to be wary of adapting the grand conclusions of art critics, or literary ones, for that matter, to the latterday fortunes of the rest of us. For many of us there will be some falling-away eventually in abilities we have developed over our lifetime – we may get worse even at washing-up, cleaning our teeth, tidying up – though that falling-away will probably be neither dramatic nor likely to throw retrospective light on the activities of our youth. Nor are such changes likely to operate as the vanguard to future generations. Many old people do drop the work and preoccupations of their earlier life and genuinely retire into developing new interests and learning new skills, even discovering new talents. I have friends who have taken up ballroom dancing and etching and Latin and the cello in old age. It is perhaps only at the extremes of artistic production, and then only occasionally, that questions about late style are at issue. I would love to be 'preternaturally aware of the present' and 'full of memory' at the same time, as Said prescribes, but I suspect he is writing about the survival of extraordinary capacities in extraordinary people and then how such people might go on to produce something beyond themselves. And when their late work does break with their early work, as it did with Beethoven and Titian and to some extent with Cézanne, to the point of displaying a startlingly new freshness and excitement (conceivably connected with the loss of hearing in the first and alterations to their eyesight in the other two), it may appear to be so ahead of its time as to constitute a rebarbative kind of modernism, introducing possibilities that only an entirely new generation will be able to recognise and exploit.

It is this relation of the work of a few exceptional artists to their own generation, and then to the next, that is crucial here, I think. And the paradoxical aspects of that are that such work may be produced in solitude, and that its powerful influence on future generations may easily be inadvertent and accidental, just as its creation may have happened quite outside the boundaries set by fashion and what is admired at the time. There have been suggestions that the apparent simplicity and free use of paint in some of Titian's late work, for instance, may be the result of these paintings being unfinished. It could also be argued that there is a characteristic carelessness in the old, which might account for a painter's being newly prepared to release quantities of unfinished work into the world.

*

There is another paradox. Many old people struggle with an impaired short-term memory while reporting memories of their childhood that have the 'vividness and brightness of a dream'. Esther Salaman, in her *A Collection of Moments*, a study of what she calls 'involuntary memories' and the uses writers have made of them, suggests that these rare, unexpected memories that come to us unbidden, out of the blue, may be richly, almost miraculously revealing of moments and themes from our childhood. They may come drenched in feeling, to the point where they light up far more than the moments they draw on. These, Salaman suggests, are more often experienced by the old than by the young. She gives as examples Harriet Martineau and Edwin Muir, both writers for whom such late and sudden memories made possible the accounts of childhood they wrote at the ends of their lives. Salaman also writes about the Russian writer Aksakov, who was born in 1791 and died when he was nearly sixty-eight, having written all his life about the countryside and sport and his family. He had experienced involuntary memories since childhood, almost as electric shocks or fits, but never felt able to make use of them in his writing, though he tried more than once to start a 'Childhood' and gave up. Suddenly, in old age, when he was nearly blind, he was able to write *Years of Childhood*, one of the greatest memoirs ever written, confident at last of possessing the evidence he needed.

If questions about 'late style' and what it might mean are hardly likely to affect most of us in old age, there are ways in which those questions do reverberate for us all. There is, first, promise or its opposite, how we think of our youth and how we narrate our lives to ourselves: what went wrong or right and when; which were the moments of change or the moments when possibilities for change were missed, passed over? Are there pangs or serious griefs because of what we gave up, forgot, ignored? What about those expectations that may have been misjudged in the first place or confounded, or even fulfilled or exceeded? What do we tell ourselves about our achievements, our failures, what might have been? How much depends on success, acceptance, encouragement, opportunity? It is not simply that hope and promise fade, it is that they are overtaken and submerged by what actually happens to us. My father's promise became pretty shadowy as he turned to earning his living as a teacher and marvelling uneasily at the three daughters he often seemed surprised to have produced. And when we are old it may not be that our gifts or energies or desires have faded or atrophied, but that we have learned our lesson and are no longer able or willing to pit ourselves against our contemporaries, let alone those younger and more energetic than we are.

There is no question but that the old lose out in any popularity stakes. Sometimes I wonder what it would be like to wake up cleverer or suddenly to discover talents you never had before. Would it really mean that at this late stage we had to up our game, change our lives, research into parasitology or the importance of 'shroud leakage modelling in multistage turbine flow calculations', as some of the graduates of my old college seem to have done, or run the marathon?

*

Old age comes late, but then we were always late for some things. I was late for the First World War and the worst of the Depression. We are always late for our parents' youth, since our arrival necessarily coincided with their pretending at the very least that they were grown-up now. Writing about my parents in my old age has had the effect of making me for-give them their trespasses. I could picture them: these charming students, grappling with a baby and marriage and careers and money and cooking and a home. Far too young for such things, I find myself thinking now. No wonder they weren't perfect parents. Yet by the time I was conscious of them as an adult, it was already late, almost too late for sym-pathy, friendship, equality. I would always be out of step with them. And now it's late again. I tell myself that I want to stay alive for at least another ten years in order to see all my grandchildren into their adult lives. But it will still be late for me and for them. They will have come into the world too late to believe in my youth, to know quite what we have in common and what we don't, and for me it will just be late. I will be marked by my lateness, never sure if this is my time or theirs or whether it really does belong to all of us.

Simone de Beauvoir quotes from Montaigne's writing about old age and ends with his gloomy aside, 'Never a soul is to be seen, or very few, who in growing old does not take on a sour and mouldy smell.' De Beauvoir adds:

I admire the way Montaigne tosses all those conventional and comforting clichés overboard, refusing to accept any sort of deterioration as progress or to consider the mere accumulation of years as enriching. But there is a curious paradox in his case, that may have escaped Montaigne himself, though it is strikingly apparent to the reader: the *Essais* become richer and richer, more and more intimate, original and profound as the book's author grows older. He would not have been able to write these fine, sour, disillusioned pages on old age when he was thirty.

10

Clutter

I gave about fifty boxes of family letters to the Women's Library in the East End last year. It was a good moment. Several shelves were suddenly emptied. The letters go back to the end of the seventeenth century and the first stirrings of Unitarianism, and many of them are written by women to other women, though there is a family tradition – threaded through two centuries – of women politely, if unwisely, asking a man for advice and getting a great deal of it – by return – often thunderously delivered and admonishing. This may be about what to read, about science or music or education or religion. I have written about some of these letter writers elsewhere, so I will leave them in their library vault for now.

I should admit, however, that I kept back thirteen letters Karl Marx wrote in the 1850s and 60s to my great-grandfather, who was once his editor and became his friend, and I sold them at a swanky London auction house.

The irony of making a profit from Marx's letters and then, within a month or so, parting with a good deal of it to the Credit Crunch, or the Economic Downturn, or indeed to the End of Capitalism, was not entirely lost on me. But I am so pleased to be shot of them that I have barely dwelt on my brief gain or sudden loss. I need no longer worry when people who know what they're talking about ask me questions about those letters and I can't even find them, let alone answer the questions. The shelves are completely filled up again, however, and I am back with the problem of clearing my remaining clutter. By now it's not just mine, but the selected flotsam of about twenty dead relations as well.

I hear that there are people who spend quite a lot of money renting storage containers in warehouses on the outskirts of London (you see them disconcertingly advertised as Self Storage), where they deposit possessions they can't yet bring themselves to give away or throw away. I also hear that quite a lot of people visit their containers at weekends – as you might your elderly mother or your allotment – in order to comfort and reassure their discarded sofas and armchairs that what they are experiencing is only their old age, not death itself. I always want to be more hard-hearted than that, but the truth is that I've usually failed to reduce, let alone eliminate, my clutter, and though occasionally I manage to evince a ruthless hatred for it all, that doesn't as a rule transform itself into getting rid of anything. I believe you can hire declutterers to do it for you: professionals, who would instantly recognise the seriously poor quality of what fills my cupboards and drawers and shelves. But I haven't the courage to let them into the house to examine it, and I know that I'd find it hard to abide by their view of what needed to go and what could stay. In 'Missing Things', a poem Vernon Scannell wrote not long before he died, he reminds himself that 'Already I begin to miss the things/ I'll leave behind', that his possessions are 'a part of what I am'. Yet those relics, those orphan objects, acquire such a forlorn, unwanted look once their owner has died – reason enough to divest ourselves of them now, before it is too late. The trouble with all this attempted tidying, though, is this. I grew up being so much better at it than my parents that I relaxed, told myself that in this respect, if in no other, I was competent, up to scratch, better than average. But I learned soon enough that this faith in my organising powers was misplaced in relation to most of the rest of the world. Other people, I discovered, had learned how to do these things as children, from their parents. I had only learned how not to do them.

From time to time a message pops up on my computer screen offering to declutter things for me there. I refuse the offer at once, click it into oblivion, fearful that Microsoft's criteria for what should be cleared out might be just as wrong-headed as Microsoft's spelling and grammar. So, sitting in there somewhere (the ether, the hard disk, some virtual storage space), causing no bother and collecting no dust, are records of precious moments sent to me as email attachments out of the past and youth of two people who had never heard of emails and regarded typewriters as alarmingly new-fangled.

I'm moved by these unexpected glimpses of two loved and important adults in my life, whose younger selves I could only imagine. From the friend of a friend I suddenly catch sight of my father four years before I was born. He was living in Berlin. It was 1928 and he was twenty-three. You could see him as rather frantically living the last months of his youth, before he had to settle down to earn a living, marry, have children; though he may not have seen it like that. Walter Leigh, the gifted English composer who died in the Second World War, met my father in Berlin. They were almost exactly the same age and may easily have met before that at Cambridge. Leigh wrote to his sister in England, 'I have run Collet to earth, and had lunch with him the other day. He is enjoying Berlin very much, practising hard all day and going to the opera in the evening. A queer bird, chiefly in appearance and manner, being one of those who never buy clothes and only just brush their hair. But nice and clever.' He was still not buying clothes and not brushing his thick white hair at all thoroughly in his late eighties. More surprising is the news that he went to the opera every night in Berlin. I like to think of him enjoying himself, but I am also made sad by that particular fact about him, for he rarely went to operas when I knew him, and must have relinquished that passion, along with several others, when he married and struggled, as he always did, to make a living out of music. Walter Leigh was a young man of insight. In the following year, he wrote again to his sister about my father:

He is a very nice fellow, and I am glad to know him better: but he is odd, having lost his mother, I gather, at an early age. Also he is the youngest son of an old father: he has, I believe, a brother of 40! The result is that he is very self-reliant and zielbewusst [which I think means 'purposeful'] and so forth, but curiously careless of his material surroundings.

Also nestling on the 'desktop' of my computer are one hundred typed pages of the diary written by an uncle of mine, originally by hand. Arthur was one of my mother's four brothers, my father's old schoolfriend and the person who introduced my parents to each other. Born in 1904 into a Jewish family living in a Hertfordshire village, he kept a diary throughout his life, though intermittently. It covered his schooldays at Bedales, where he was head boy; his time at Cambridge; then the Second World War, when he worked as a country GP, deeply objecting to the war itself and writing a striking account of a frightening London air raid; and finally the months of illness leading to his death in 1964. The diaries are remarkably candid and lively, but also memorable for his treatment of two important events in his young life: the death of his identical twin brother, Edward, when they were nine, and the death of a much revered and admired mother when he was twenty-one.

Arthur was a kind, charming and humorous man, sometimes cast within this rather self-reverential and puritanical family as nice but naughty and a good deal too interested in drink and women. He was plagued all his life by a ferocious tic, which seemed to impede neither his work nor his driving, nor his interest in drink and women. His entries about these two catastrophic deaths may begin to explain that tic. Here he is, recalling the moment of his twin's death:

For thirty-eight years I have been wondering whether or not to write down what I am writing now. During this time I expected to meet someone who I could tell it to, to get the thing out of my system, but I haven't met such a person, & if I had it would still be in my system just the same. If it does good to tell your things to someone else, perhaps it does good to write these things down.

On Christmas Eve 1913 my twin brother Edward and I lay dying with pneumonia in the night nursery at Barley. We were both delirious, but he was worse than I was, & clearly didn't know how bad he was, or I hope not. We both came to our senses every now & again & in one of those moments he called to me. He called me by a name used in our own special private language & he kept on calling. I knew he just wanted me to answer his name using the language again. There was a blasted under-nurse in the room & I felt ashamed to use the rather silly name I had for him because I hadn't the courage to do it in her hearing. I was afraid of her ridicule. So I pretended to be asleep. He kept on calling & I never answered, so he stopped & died later that night.

Since then I have learned to know that if I had answered him he would not have died. Soon after that night I got acute heart failure & knew I would die if the nurse didn't read to me. I felt absolutely certain that that, and that only would save my life. I gasped for her to read something to me – anything, and she did. I got my breath back soon and then began to recover.

His son William, who assembled and typed out the diary, believes that this death affected Arthur deeply for the whole of his life, and that Edward, his dead twin, may be the implied reader of the diary, which is sometimes written as if for someone who would know nothing of the events it recounts. So that when he writes about the Second World War, for instance, he writes as someone explaining its horrors to a reader who is not there, not implicated. Here is his entry for 17 April 1941:

Yesterday I went to London & was caught in the worst air-raid London has ever had. I dined with the Proctors in Tryon St. The warnings went & the bombs began to crash around. Soon the sky was all glowing with fires. At about 12.30 a.m. I drove over to Dennis Cohen's house in Church St., Chelsea as he was alone. The attacks seemed to consist of endless dive-bombing which makes a soul-freezing noise followed by the most shattering crashes. We foolishly undressed & went to bed in his dugout but things were so bad we got up & had to dress in the dark as the black-outs had been blown down. Looking out of the window we saw at least five nearby houses burning. His house has huge glass French windows and as I was looking out through one of them a land mine went

off 100 yards away. I was blown across the room on my
stomach completely winded. All the windows in the
house were broken & fittings strewn all over the place.
Dennis was alright as he wasn't by the window. Somehow
I got no cuts at all. We wandered about in the dark looking at the fires for some time & there were dozens of
them. The sky was blazing. I then went out to the Cancer
Hospital & muscled in with the doctors taking in the
casualties. There were a lot of them & I worked there till
6.30. The roads were littered with glass & timber & bits
of houses & where the land mine had dropped a whole
block of houses was completely smashed up. I drove
home at 8.00 & had to get straight to work as Browne [his
practice partner] went to London. The wireless said it was
the biggest raid ever & the damage & casualties were very
considerable.

The nervous strain was very great. Every time you
hear some bombs go off safely distant, a new dive-
bomber whine starts & you have to tense up again. When
it goes on for about 8 hours the nerves get a bit tattered.
I find myself much more afraid of being killed than of
being hurt . . .

P.S. The land mine was proved to be two, interlocked.

A plaque has just been fixed to the wall of the Fire Station,
in memory – sixty-eight years after 'The Wednesday', as it
came to be called – of the seven auxiliary firemen who died
in that air raid. Perhaps some of their great-grandchildren
have arranged for it to be put there. I pass that house made

mostly of glass almost every day on my way to and from swimming. It was built between 1934 and 1936 by the Expressionist architects Erich Mendelsohn and Serge Chermayeff, and it is still probably the most beautiful 'modern' house in Chelsea.

I didn't know Arthur's mother Nina, who was my maternal grandmother. She died nearly eight years before I was born. I grew up in awe of her, nonetheless, though over the years I began to wonder whether there hadn't been something cold, ungiving and probably manipulative about this allegedly beautiful and talented woman, famous for her Hebrew scholarship and her rather syrupy poems. She died at forty-eight, after five awful years of bowel cancer. Those years and their ending clearly made a lasting impression on her children. My mother and her sister, the youngest children of the family, had been kept in the dark about their mother's condition, and when she died they were instantly sent away from home, something they raged at until their dying days. Her sons were allowed to know the truth and even to say goodbye. Arthur was twenty-one when he recorded, flatly and piously, what that was like:

Mother said good-bye to us this morning. She is unconscious now & they are applying drugs to keep away pain. It was a terrible moment but she was so dignified and still the same masterly character. Her main wish is that we don't marry out. After a talk with Dad some time ago I am convinced she is right & that it is a mistake to marry out.

I felt I simply couldn't get my tongue to work, & just muttered some rubbish. If I could have had a good cry like Sis, it would have been better but it is a physical impossibility for me. She said she would give my love to Edward if she met him. A day never passes without my remembering him, we practically shared minds.

The house is very gloomy but it has been expected for so long that it is not such a sudden shock as it might have been.

And the next day, he wrote:

Mother died this morning at 9.40. She did not regain consciousness but made a terrible fight for it. Dad passed a terrible night in the room & was continually worried with the idea that she might be feeling it, but he says he is sure she was really quite unconscious. In the afternoon Aunt Dorothy, Uncle Fred & Michel came down. Uncle Michel looked very distraught and is staying some days I believe, which I consider a very good thing. Ruth & Esther have gone off to stay with Aunt Isabelle for a week.

I only realise now what an absolute centre to the family she was. Am feeling most bedraggled. Next vac we are all going to scatter about, & Dad will probably take a ruck-sack thro' France & be free for a bit. Nurse Potts says she was the bravest & most patient woman she has ever known, & that it has been a privilege & an education to know her. To the last she was taking an interest in every-thing, especially the Women's Institute. The funeral is next Wednesday. She has been the greatest sort of success, & it will be hard to live up to her example, but it's got to be done. No man could be so patient and brave. I couldn't. Dead, dead, dead. I can't imagine it, it's impossible. No one will ever know. The whole of existence is based on that one ignorance. I feel a sort of restless madness. It will be awful trying to work again tomorrow.

Less than three years later, Arthur wrote in his diary again:

What I wrote earlier about mother I now know to be wrong. What's more I knew it then really. She was the worst mother conceivable. I was continually in mortal dread of her and spent most of the early days doing anything to keep out of her sight. As a teacher she had no patience & hit us about in a most disgraceful way. Hebrew lessons meant nothing but fear & trembling for all of us. That's what's made me the nervous wreck that I am. I never once in twenty years remember her calling me 'dear' or anything of the sort. In fact, I can remember practically nothing but scolding. It destroyed my self-confidence & made me feel I was less than nobody which now in truth it has caused me to become.

One of the greatest surprises of my life was when on first going to school I found that the masters did not come & thrash you over the face & curse you for everything. No wonder we liked school. I still feel the terror of her presence. Why did she do it? In other respects she was wise enough & always charming to those outside the home circle. Very likely she thought it best for us, I don't know. Anyway she whispered to me she was sorry, when she was dying, but I couldn't answer.

Her children are all dead now. There is no one to take her part, defend her. Perhaps she could not forgive Arthur for staying alive when Edward died. Another of those destructive traditions that families like mine go in for has it that 'Edward was the cleverest of them all'.

You could say that their sock drawers were significant for both my parents. My father kept the Marx letters in his, while my mother always tidied hers just before guests arrived. Hers actually contained stockings and tights as well as socks, and I don't think she really envisaged her guests snooping among her clothes or recoiling in horror as they did so. It was a symbolic act, meant to stand for more visible manifestations of order, which were, as they are for so many of us, much harder to handle. I acquired the Marx letters, without the socks, when my father died and I was already in my sixties, so disposing of them and the other family letters was relatively painless; and in a year or so they will be catalogued, and I could visit them then if I wanted to, just to see how they're getting on without me.

Ridding myself of things I've had since childhood or for a great number of years is much harder. My childhood and my youth are gone, over, and I don't in the least wish them back, though I am surprised by how interested I can become, as I peer through cloudy, smudged windows at the childhood and

youth of those I knew only as adults. Among the confused
miscellany of memories that fills my head are all those other
people's memories: *their* records, *their* diaries, *their* struggles
to sort out the relics of a lifetime. And if I find myself clinging to objects and photographs, it is not so much because
they remind me of the past or bring it back, but because I
use them as aids or prompts in order to help me construct
a private narrative I sometimes like to recite to myself about
my own life, but also about the lives of people I once knew,
who are dead now. Mementoes are there instead of memory,
or to provoke memories.

For instance, I have just found a little clutch of photographs taken, I think, in 1953 when, with two friends from
university, I rented a room on the edge of Saint-Tropez in
the South of France for five shillings a week each, figs,
tomatoes and wine thrown in. I don't know who took the
photographs, but they're small and low-grade, barely deci-
pherable. Saint-Tropez wasn't known to celebrities in those
days, though somebody once saw Orson Welles emerging
from a doorway and disappearing into the night, and Jean-
Louis Barrault and his wife had been seen sipping Cinzano
in the café on the front, so that Cinzano with a piece of
lemon peel in it swiftly became and remained for some
years my favourite alcoholic drink. I remember only one
hotel in the town, a small one built like an igloo, and the
beaches beyond the port were long and sandy and empty.
You could swim and sunbathe there with nothing on and
never be seen or disturbed. Outside the house where we
stayed a thin, almost naked man and a small stocky woman

in a vest and shorts worked all day long to produce their figs and tomatoes and wine (their heads are missing in the photograph I have of them); and living in a boat on the inlet behind the house was an actor and producer called Roger Blin, a strange, unsmiling man with short arms and dry, spiky black hair, who had just discovered Beckett's *Waiting for Godot* and had put it on in Paris, where it was a success. Roger Blin fell in love with Sasha Moorsom, the beauty among us, and when we returned to London she told Peter Hall all about Beckett. Just under two years later, *Waiting for Godot* was put on at the Arts Theatre near Leicester Square, with Peter Woodthorpe as one of the tramps. He and I had appeared in a university Russian production of Pushkin's *Boris Godunov.*

That's what I mean by photographs working to stimulate or provoke memories. Suddenly that whole hot summer month comes back, our walks home along the coast road from the town at night, the heat still simmering and the crickets singing for all they were worth. At the beginning there were just us three girls. But then we were visited by Nick Tomalin and David Gillies, two friends who had come all the way there on a single motorbike. A doctor given to threatening suicide put his tent up in the garden, and another friend tumbled out of a bus in the market square, shoeless and moneyless, having left home after a row when her mother discovered a Dutch cap in her knicker drawer. She got a job in a local restaurant, I remember, by claiming that she could speak Provençal. There was a young Frenchman there too, who gave me my only smoke of pot, and I believe

I threw away what I thought of as the stub rather than handing it back to him as I should have done.

I've found lots of things I thought I'd lost in my current attempt to tidy up my life, but I'm still searching for my copies of *I.F. Stone's Weekly*, that extraordinary one-man radical news-sheet that Izzy Stone wrote and edited from Washington for nineteen years, assisted only by his wife, Esther. I can't believe I would have thrown them away, even if I never really expected to settle down to read them again. Somewhere I have almost ten years' worth of them, starting from about 1965, when I first met Izzy and Esther. During the years when I worked for a series of publishers I was responsible for a book of his selected articles, and we became friends. What he principally wanted from me, it turned out, was information about somewhere he and his wife could go dancing in the afternoon, a *thé dansant*. He seemed to imagine that there would be one such place on every street corner in London and that I would naturally spend a good many of my afternoons dancing in them. I failed him on this, though I remember traipsing round Soho and Mayfair frantically searching for somewhere. Finally I remembered the Dorothy Tearooms in Cambridge, which I'd heard of but never visited, and the Stones took up my suggestion and the train from Liverpool Street and waltzed more than one afternoon away there.

I was also, I suddenly remember, instrumental in arranging for him to have lunch with Isaiah Berlin at the Savoy Grill. Isaiah and Isidor had never met, but they fell upon one another like the oldest of friends, and talked nonstop and

pretty well simultaneously for several hours, leaving most of
their meal to be returned to the kitchen. Both were the sons
of Russian Jewish immigrants, though their lives, one
grandly liberal in England, the other contentiously radical in
America, could hardly have been more different. If their
interests and some of their friends overlapped, their politics,
their families and the social worlds they inhabited did so far
less.

We saw Izzy and Esther once or twice during the seventies, when they'd given up the *Weekly* because of his bad eyes
and unreliable heart. He taught himself Greek during those
last years, and a year before he died in 1989 he brought out
The Trial of Socrates, which emerged from the 'study of freedom of thought in human history' that he'd planned to write
in his retirement. This took him first to the English revolu-
tion of the seventeenth century, then further back to the
Protestant Reformation, and finally to ancient Athens and
what is often thought of as the second most famous trial in
history. It also furnished him with questions: 'How could the
trial of Socrates have happened in so free a society? How
could Athens have been so untrue to itself?' His answers
were detailed and scholarly and they relied on his knowledge
of Greek; but the book was also written in response to the
events of his times and his disappointment during the 1980s
with what was happening to America.

Is all this clutter 'a part of what I am'? Can I begin to make
out a narrative of my life by wading through all this stuff that
surrounds me? When I was in my forties I read several books

by feminist and post-structuralist writers which insisted on the constructedness of persons, on its being an illusion to think that we pre-exist the language and the culture that form us, or that there is, even, a single, continuous, identifiable person there at all. We have become who we are, according to such a view, by barnacling versions of ourselves around our names and other arbitrary signs and definitions bestowed on us by the particular world and time we inhabit, perpetually trying out possibilities and identities, and we must think of our selves, therefore, as fragmented and inherently unstable. I think I believed that for a bit too, or something quite like it – a more Marxist version of it, perhaps, which made more of the effect on us as individuals of class and money and our relation to forms of power and powerlessness. But I don't believe it quite so unequivocally any more. Nor did Simone de Beauvoir by the time she wrote *Old Age*, though she seemed to be saying something else, I suppose, with that famous first line of *The Second Sex*, 'One is not born, but rather becomes a woman.' I don't think that quite fits with her later insistence that:

> All old people's neuroses have their source in their childhood or their adolescence. It is easy to understand why they return so willingly to their childhood – they are possessed by it. They recognise themselves in their childhood because – even if they have chosen to ignore it for a while – it has never ceased to inhabit them. And there is another reason. Life consists of going beyond oneself, of self-transcendence. But when people are very old, this

transcendence comes up sharply against death. The old person attempts to give his existence a foundation by reclaiming his birth or at least his earliest years.

As usual, I'm not ready to go quite as far as she does, and I'm never sure about transcendence of any kind, or that I even know quite what it means. It's not so much that I feel possessed or explained by my childhood, or that I need it or recognise myself in it in quite the way de Beauvoir suggests. Nor do I find myself invoking the values of those years as likely to be authentic in ways that later ones are not.

I remember, in fact, feeling quite pleased when my childhood was over. But in order to make any sense of my old age, of now, I do look for some kind of continuity, for one thing having happened after another and before something else. I want to think of time as having passed in an orderly fashion, appropriately filled, with no glaring gaps or lost good things to match the gaps in my memory of it all, nor too much evidence of waste or emptiness, of sleeping away life's possibilities. There are huge gaps in my remembering, however, and in a cavalier way I imagine those blank times as explained by repetition, by more or less the same sort of thing happening day after day, week after week. But the stretches I've characterised as repetitive, monotonous, featureless, without remarkable incident, are also hard to remember even in their regularity. I would find it hard to say that between 1969 and 1975, for instance, when I was teaching in a large London school, I spent the week more or less in this way, and weekends more or less in that. Though now

I come to think of it, there are habits and patterns I remember: dashing into Waitrose on Friday on my way home from school, and my parents visiting on Sunday afternoons, and organising clean clothes for everyone on Sunday evenings, though that last bit could easily be a fiction.

And all those years of teaching. Faces, voices, moments jump out at me. The boy whose woolly hat I recklessly whipped off when he threatened another boy, and he turned on me to suggest that he and I fight it out publicly in the playground; the small girl who took my arm as we walked along a corridor, obliging me to bend down in order to hear her, and told me chattily that her father had murdered her mother, and was doing time for it; and the headmaster explaining the morning after I'd been promoted that he'd told the governors I didn't need the job. He was sure that as I had a husband to support me I only worked for 'pin money'.

A few years ago I went once a week to Russian evening classes in that school. I sat at the window of the classroom next to the one where I used to teach forty years ago. The garden outside has been taken in hand; the whole building has. As my Russian classes were in the evening it was hard to remember or imagine the place full of swaggering, noisy, friendly children, some of them smoking among the now glorious rhododendrons. The inglorious bike shed has been demolished, and there are potted plants, miraculously unmolested, wherever you look. Inside the school, along the walls of the corridors, there are portraits of children in uniform, with captions explaining how they've met and exceeded 'targets' of various kinds. There was no uniform in the old days, and I don't remember the word 'target' crossing our lips, though I do remember worrying about the difference between 'aims' and 'objectives' and wondering why you needed to have both. The whole school is festooned in captions now, written in fancy fonts, offering moral guidance and lists of particular contemporary virtues: achievement, effort, excellence, leadership are high on the list of good things to go for. Not much talk of subtlety, humour, negative capability, sympathy. Nowadays you can just 'achieve', you're even expected to, without specifying what exactly you're achieving (a perfectly good verb wilfully made intransitive).

As I sat in that classroom, with its whiteboard and computerised audiovisual aids that often didn't work, rather as the blackboard and its rubber and supply of chalk would sometimes let you down in the old days, I was more aware of the passing of time, of my time as well as time in general, than of the continuities. But I was also returned to childhood, to my own schooldays, to the drumbeat anxieties of classrooms, as places where you can so easily make a fool of yourself. Teachers are always vulnerable in classrooms, but so — as I was reminded all over again — are their students. And even now in my Russian class I could feel sick with worry when I knew my turn to answer a question was coming up.

Memory may be rich in invention, but the material it uses for its invention must come from somewhere and have some reliability, so that it becomes of considerable interest in itself. And there does seem to be a kind of will in us, there from birth, which directs us and holds us together and starts us on the road to distinguishing ourselves decisively from the other people around us. Without memory, that would be inconceivable. My old friend Richard Wollheim wrote *Germs* during the last eight years or so of his life. It is arguably his best book and it is mostly, though not entirely, about his first eight years. He wrote it some time after emerging from a long psychoanalysis, so that he'd already established connections between his childhood and the more obtrusive or bizarre obsessions of his grown-up self: his terror of drowning, his indifference to music and, most persistent of all, his intolerance of certain smells, especially the smell of newspapers. This horror of newspapers was something we all took into account when he visited us. And though I never saw him retch at the sight of one, he adamantly assured us that he would if there were one any-where in the room, even if it was hidden. At the end of *Germs* he tells the story that originally set off this dread of newspapers and their smell, recalled from when he was two and a half. He remembered his older brother spitting pel-lets on to their nanny's newspaper which were made from scraps of the newspaper itself that he'd mixed with his saliva. The front page of that newspaper was full of photo-graphs of Queen Alexandra, who had just died: so that she, the photographs, the newspaper, were 'desecrated by spit, and smell, and the signs of disease'. One curiosity of this early memory and its lifelong effect on him is the surpris-ingly undesecrated nanny and the relatively fleeting and unblamed presence in it of his older brother in Wollheim's reliving, retelling and interpretation of it. He remembered that his brother had signalled that he, the younger brother, aged two and a half, ought really to own up to the deed. He writes of envying this brother throughout his childhood and he appears to have distanced himself from him as an adult. I wonder whether, within the welter of vivid and precise details that memory provides – the main thing, the person or event or object holding the source of all the pain or all the delight of such a moment – may still refuse to emerge from its position, cowering, as if afraid of its own power, behind metaphors that are simultaneously infected by and protective of that important source.

Helen Small, whom I've mentioned before, and who has written about old age from a philosophical point of view rather than a personal one, was less than forty when she started writing *The Long Life*, and her purpose was not to imagine it so much as to contemplate old age as a spectacle that provokes thoughts about what a life is, and especially what a good life might be thought to be. So old age is implicated for her in what literature has made of human tragedy, heroism and virtue and their opposites. I'd like to think that very old criminals, war criminals say, but others too, were treated more leniently, even let off some or all of their punishment. This might imply that they were too old to change or were unlikely to cause much damage at this stage, or that their dying in prison, unable to endure it all, would be an embarrassment for the rest of us. Villainy itself might be

thought of, then, as weakening with age, reduced, attenuated: vice diluted rather as virtue and perspicacity may be
thought to be. In fact, it seems that more old people, women
as well as men, are currently incarcerated than ever before.
It is a growth area for the prison service. And the wonderfully named Bernard Madoff, the American swindler, has just
been sentenced in his seventies to 150 years. Making off with
so much of other people's money at his age seems to be
worth more than two of his lifetimes.

Helen Small is concerned to conceptualise the end of a
life, the old part, in relation to how we think of a whole life
over time, how we value it or regret it, or value and regret
bits of it. Does old age reward wisdom, punish ignorance,
carelessness, cruelty, or press home the sheer randomness
and luck of health and happiness, the accidents of misfortune? Here she is towards the end of her explorations: old
age has repercussions, 'for what we deem to be a good life,
how we measure happiness, what we think a person is, when
we think we are at our best, what we consider thinking can
and cannot achieve.'

It seems to me that the real problem about old age is
precisely that it does come at the end of a life, so that
whatever it throws up is always read off in relation to deterioration and then to death, while also serving as an emblem
or summary of a whole life. Tolstoy's Ivan Ilyich (who isn't
old, in fact, just dying) and Shakespeare's King Lear are
watched in extremis, so we're bound to expect those last
moments to present us with the essence of the person they
have been: Ilyich is, for Tolstoy, a culpably conventional and

acquiescent man, unable to feel or respond to love, whose terrible illness and death are condign punishment for his obdurate, wasteful ordinariness. King Lear becomes vulnerable, suffering, human, ordinary too, and yet more than a king. To some extent his ending wipes out the arrogance and foolishness and grandiosity of his earlier life, though it is also their consequence.

Yet old age might be quite differently valued, as just one way of experiencing life, if only we knew it was temporary and that we were to return afterwards to – at the very least – a period of relatively vigorous mental and physical health, and were also to have a limited vista of time ahead of us that would allow for change. This would not be so much a matter of benefiting from the elixir of life, or a homecoming after exile 'from the expressive freedoms of youth', as Small puts it, but just the possibility of a future of unspecified duration (though we have that already, I suppose) and with rather less evidence than is usually the case of most things getting worse. Then, we might think of ourselves as tasting varieties of life that other people experience earlier and even perhaps for the whole of their lives: pain, physical and mental disability, loneliness, poverty, sadness.

I remember my early forties as unhappy and curiously terminal, more like old age in some ways than my seventies have been. The end of youth was tangibly present in every aspect of my life, and there were times when I found it hard to think about or believe in a future, or at any rate in a future that might offer change and interest and happiness. I felt rather as Chekhov's Uncle Vanya does:

I'm forty-seven. Suppose I live to be sixty, that's another thirteen years. It's a long time. How will I live through those thirteen years? What shall I do, how shall I fill them? Oh you must understand, you must . . . If only it was possible somehow to live the rest of one's life in a new way. You'd wake up one clear, quiet morning and feel that you were going to start life all over again, that the past was forgotten, blown away, like smoke.

His old friend Astrov, the doctor, rebukes him for expecting to be happy. They should both be thinking about future generations. I felt rebuked too. I had children for whom life really was full of promise. How could I expect it to be full of promise for me too? Yet just ahead, as it turned out, were the years when I finally found what it was I wanted to do with my life.

You could say, though, that there's been a dark side to growing older from the very beginning. I think of Janice Galloway remembering the first signs of puberty – when it was still called growing 'up' – in her extraordinary memoir of childhood, *This Is Not About Me*. 'This was no respecter of persons, this change,' she writes, 'it was ruthless, relentless and not done yet.' I certainly hated growing up, most especially reminders that I was 'becoming a woman', though I think my parents tactfully refrained from that particular brand of encouragement. Then there was the grim boundary line of twenty-one, and after that all those other moments when you'd passed the point of being unusually young, or just young, or young at all. A friend of mine, who is now forty-five and enjoying his life rather less than he has in the past, remarked to me recently that the secret for him was to be forty-five and not to remind himself, even occasionally, that in five years' time he will be fifty. Perhaps there is a lesson there for someone in their seventies too. I am not yet, after all, nearly as old as I'm quite likely to become.

Montaigne doesn't stint on the discomforts, the overeating, the indigestion, the physical and mental losses of old age. But he is tolerant of them too and even welcomes some of these fallings-away, as distractions from thinking about death; and because some of them could be said to make the prospect of death more welcome than it might otherwise be:

> God shows mercy to those from whom he takes away life a little at a time: that is the sole advantage of growing old; the last death which you die will be all the less total and painful: it will only be killing off half a man, or a quarter. Look: here is a tooth which has just fallen out with no effort or anguish: it had come to the natural terminus of its time. That part of my being, as well as several other parts, are already dead: others are half-dead, including those which were, during the vigour of my youth, the most energetic and uppermost. This is how I drip and drain away from myself. What animal-stupidity it would be if my intellect took for the whole of that collapse the last topple of an already advanced decline. I hope that mine will not.

Shakespeare must have read Montaigne by the time he wrote *King Lear*. He certainly could have done, since the first English translation, by John Florio, came out in 1603, two years before the play. Old age is so physical for them both, so much lived in the head and the body as well as in the world; and both of them died in their fifties, which I suppose people would have regarded then as a ripe old age.

Why do I regularly forget the endings of stories, films, plays? Who dies, who thrives? Uncle Vanya returns to his work running the family estate. Of course he does, poor fellow, doggedly muttering 'work, work', though without much enthusiasm. I've just checked, because I'd actually forgotten whether he managed to shoot himself or to down the morphia he took from Astrov's bag. And I regularly forget, and have to check, what Tolstoy does with his novel after Anna launches herself under the train. Apart from some sarcastic sightings of Vronsky travelling in another train with his own militia in order to fight nobly for the Serbians against the Turks while, simultaneously, drowning his sorrows, Tolstoy tells us almost nothing about the effect of Anna's death on her husband, her brother, her children. Instead, he ends with Levin's spiritual turmoil, leaving probably the best novel ever written on a note of bathos, as far as I'm concerned. No wonder I had forgotten. I do hope Levin will go back to running his estate eventually too, even to grumbling about the peasants, but it seems quite likely that he'll spend the rest of his life wrestling with God and giving his wife a hard time, rather as Tolstoy did. My attention does seem to wander at the point when films or plays or novels are winding down or summing up. I find myself skirting conclusions, ignoring the moral that is usually lurking there, implicit in how it all ends. I think of those ominous gaps at the ends of obituaries. The full, energetic life, awash in achievements and wives and children. Then suddenly nothing for ten years or more at the end. What sort of ending has that been? Boredom, illness, dementia, solitude? No, I don't want things to end and I am wary of how endings come about and the meanings we're supposed to take from them.

It is their endlessness that I particularly warm to in television soaps, the way their plots have no grand finales (though there are lots of minor ones) and their characters are allowed to remake themselves, become nicer or nastier than we thought them, lose and acquire spouses, parents, siblings, friends, children, jobs. People get over things in soaps and simply embark on the next bit of their lives, another storyline, another sequence of episodes. They seem not to carry the marks, as we would, of betrayals and fires and murders, or even of black eyes, for very long. Think of Ken Barlow, once a nineteen-year-old swot, then a student, and, since then, multiply married, sheepishly adulterous, swooning to Wagner, reading the *Guardian*, with children and grandchildren we didn't know even existed appearing all the time, and on he goes, sometimes a teacher, then a journalist, then suddenly serving tea and beans on toast in his pinny in Roy Cropper's café. What can it be like for him, sharing a house with Deirdre, his wife, and Blanche, his mother-in-law (now dead, and no doubt sadly missed)? How he must curse the scriptwriters.

I suppose he's just about my age, but his life has been far more varied than mine has been, even if he has spent most of it in Coronation Street. And I've spent fifty years in the same London house, after all, with no Rover's Return in which to exchange neighbourly gossip or refashion my reputation. We do have a local pub, in fact, from which my daughter and her friends were extruded more than thirty years ago for stealing an ashtray. So we've never gone back. Ken Barlow very nearly escaped to London on a barge the other day, with an actress I remember from *Dynasty*; but he got cold feet just in time, as I would have done. He's recovered from that pretty fast. I suspect that if you asked him her name he'd probably admit that he'd forgotten it by now. And how relieved that actress must be to be out of *Coronation Street* and available for Shakespearean parts again. Because when one of the characters leaves a soap, to die or to move to Manchester (if they're in *EastEnders*) or to London – or, sometimes, for a stretch inside – we can reassure ourselves, as my sensible seven-year-old granddaughter once reminded me, that the actor probably has another part in *The Bill* or *Holby City*, or is appearing in pantomime in Guildford. Actors who leave *Neighbours* usually go to London to become pop stars.

These actors are almost as multi-skilled, as I think it's called, as the characters they play. And the characters themselves change career the whole time in a way I admire and which governments are always hoping people will find it

easy to do in real life, though they don't, of course:
machine-sewing knickers one day, buying and selling in the
market the next, cutting hair, running bookies, grocers,
builders' yards, youth clubs and nightclubs, pubs, restaurants, beauty salons, garages, newsagents, minicab firms,
fish and chip shops, and so on. No retraining, and not an
MBA among them. The only teacher I can remember, apart
from Ken, is just out of prison (for kidnapping and then
incarcerating a girl who was once his pupil). Doctors come
and go, and so do the police. And the same bent lawyer
(referred to as a 'brief') always turns up when it's a matter
of defending anyone who is plainly guilty (usually Phil
Mitchell). I wonder whether the lawyer is kept on a
retainer. Quite a lot of the characters combine bar work and
other jobs with a variety of criminal pastimes. So no one is
ever unemployed for long, and no one works terribly hard,
because the weekly schedule requires them to spend their
lunch hour and most of the evening in the pub (surely, at
inordinate expense) in order to keep events and dialogue on
the move. What a comfort these programmes are in their
indefatigable determination to outlive us all.

Talking of governments and what they think and want of us,
and we of them, I spent the evening after the general election of 1997 with a group of journalists. It was the year
before I retired, and I remember that, jaded and sceptical as
most of us were, we were also cheerfully thankful that
Labour had won, that eighteen years of Tory rule had given
way to a huge Labour majority. Old people are usually

addressed by politicians as if they were unlikely to be concerned about anything but their own immediate interests, as hard-done-by pensioners or needy users of the National Health and other social services. We are not expected to care about what happens to the young or to anyone else, nor about the wars or injustices that may be entered into as much on our behalf as on other people's.

The opposite may well be the case. We have more time than we ever had in the past to read the papers and listen to the news. In fact, some of us become obsessed with the news, and watch or listen to news bulletins several times a day. We worry when hundreds of journalists are sent to Gaza or Sri Lanka for two weeks or so to cover a terrible story, which then drops right out of the news, only to be caught again from time to time on the World Service during insomniac nights. Our removal from some aspects of the world may make us feel especially vulnerable to the turbulent effects of contemporary politics, and I am even more taunted by the uselessness of my vote now than I used to be. I left the Labour Party in 1968 because of James Callaghan's desperate efforts to stop lots of Asians from coming to this country when they were thrown out of Kenya, and I can't pretend to have been active politically since then, though I have gone on several good marches. I was lightly nudged to the ground by a policeman's horse in Trafalgar Square at the time of Suez in 1956, and I went on one or two Aldermaston marches. Then there were the miners in 1984, the Iraq war in 2003 and the Israeli bombing of Gaza at the beginning of 2009. I like the company and other people shouting, but I never feel sure that demonstrations achieve very much, though the sheer scale of the anti-Iraq-war march certainly should have done.

It seems pretty likely that I will spend the rest of my life with a Tory government in power once again, and from here it's sometimes difficult to remember that the Thatcher years were even worse than these last thirteen disastrous years. What a disappointment it has all been and what appalling decisions this government has made. Far from reversing the worst policies brought in during the eighties, New Labour has confirmed and even built on most of them. Their unreassuring emphasis has been throughout on something called 'modernisation', a concept which, like 'globalisation', is deceptively weighty-seeming but actually anodyne and empty of specific meaning. We have been fobbed off with the equally meaningless offer of 'choice'. Any political idealism, any moves towards greater equality and a fairer society were systematically undermined during the eighties, with the callous destruction of the mining industry and the large city local authorities, the selling-off of council housing. Socialism, feminism, and the excitements of working towards a progressive and generous education system, were movements and ideas which meant a great deal to me and which were frustrated and rubbished during those years. I think that some of us imagined in 1997 that a little of all this Tory misrule might be undone by Labour. The railways might be renationalised, for instance, comprehensive schools might be revitalised, so that parental choice would no longer have to be invoked as the sole solution to the unevenness of

schools – because we would come to expect that the local
school was likely to be just as good as any other school.
Market forces would no longer play a part in the National
Health Service. Equal pay would be more than a piety and
become a reality, actually implemented. Free higher education would expand and become available to more and
more young people. Thousands of houses would be built that
people could afford to rent or buy. We all knew that New
Labour had nothing to do with Socialism and no truck with
equality. But we envisaged an end to the grossest inequality,
to sleaze, to reductions of the curriculum in primary and
secondary schools.

We should have realised at once that those thirteen years
would deliver very little but disappointment when it was
instantly announced that despite the Labour government's
enormous majority there would be no changes to taxation,
and very little change to anything else, for the first two years
of the new government. Much was made of 'prudence' by
Gordon Brown as Chancellor of the Exchequer, though I was
never clear who exactly was to exercise this prudence and
on whose behalf. The word must haunt him now, during
these recession-ridden, bonus-billowing, MPs'-expenses
times. I don't think that anyone that evening thought Tony
Blair was about to lead us into a wonderful new world, but
we were all sure that nothing could be worse than it had
been, and there were still a few good people in the
Parliamentary Labour Party. Thirteen years later, and most
things are worse. There have been ruinous wars in Iraq and
Afghanistan, relations between the West and the Muslim

world have deteriorated dangerously, and Tony Blair, of all people, has been put in charge of improving them.

Those of us involved in education had come to despair of politicians in the 1980s, with their introduction of the National Curriculum and League Tables and their reductive assessment schemes. None of the politicians who were then involved in education sent their children to state schools, and their contempt for such schools underpinned their policies and sowed widespread distrust of what went on in them. Independent schools have never needed to bother with the National Curriculum, after all, or with SATS. Primary schooling began during those years to be pared down to endless drilling for the SATS tests. In secondary schools, snippets of great works were compulsorily read solely in order to answer questions on them, and learning to write was reduced to formulaic essays that could be modelled and dictated by teachers (or found on the Internet) in advance. The curriculum and teaching are now determined by modes of assessment; while most public examinations are themselves determined by moves towards having them marked by computer: which circumscribes what can be asked and answered, and therefore what, minimally, must be taught and learned.

A recent report from Ofsted has noticed that some English teachers fail to get their pupils to read for pleasure or write with ease. In fact, a whole generation of teachers has been reared on the opposite of both things: on spelling and snippets and practising essay answers. There are, as there have always been, heroic teachers and flourishing schools

that have defied government restrictions and taught a rich
and broad curriculum in spite of the narrowness of what is
officially demanded and valued. The *Cambridge Primary
Review* of October 2009, which has set England's education
of young children alongside the delivery of good early education in other countries – and found us wanting – has been
summarily dismissed by the government. That same Labour
government's principal proposal for improving state education has been the setting up of academies. These are likely
to drain resources from neighbouring schools while reflect-
ing the idiosyncratic beliefs of anyone (and it really is
almost anyone) prepared to put up £2 million, which
represents no more than 5 per cent of the cost of a new
academy. James Boswell's father did not mean it as a
compliment when he described his son's friend Samuel
Johnson as a schoolmaster 'who kept a school and called it
an academy'. Schools are back as at best potential agents of
social mobility, a purpose that has survived the partial
demise of grammar schools, and has replaced any sense of
education as implicated in the delivery of social justice for
everyone's children.

And now, at the end of the first decade of the twenty-first
century, in the company of most of the rest of the world we
are deep in the worst recession of my lifetime, with mounting unemployment, and dishonesty, greed and corruption in
the City – and among politicians – flourishing on a scale no
one of my age can remember happening before. The difference in income and life possibilities between rich and poor
had already widened before the recession. That gap will grow

alarmingly in the next few years, with frightening political and social implications. The only glimmer of light on the political horizon has been the arrival on the scene of Barack Obama – graceful, clever, inspiring – in these strange, decaying times. Yet he is doubted and suspected by large sections of the British press, by journalists who have grown unused to having a gifted, humane politician in the White House and who forget, it seems, the kind of opposition with which he must contend in his own country, and the sheer impossibility of undoing the harm done by the right in America and across the world during the last eight years.

When I retired from work twelve years ago I made some resolutions. I was going to buy myself a bicycle and give up my car. I was going to see that I had all the Pevsner books on London so that I could learn about the bits of the city I didn't know, and I was going to become a good cook. I was also going to start playing the violin again, but I got out of that by lending my fiddle to a grandson who was clearly doing better with it than I ever had. So I have done none of those things, though I have done some others. I have got better at swimming and at Russian, and I have put a bird feeder in my garden, which allows me to watch, a bit obsessively, the finches and the tits that visit it and the pigeons that are maddened by it. And I really am going to sort out my house and streamline my life. I'll start with the drawers and boxes and suitcases, the ones I haven't dared to look into for years and years. I don't suppose there will be decomposing bodies in them, but there will be old clothes devoured by moths,

and objects whose uncertain charms have defeated my plans
to discard them many times in the past. Perhaps I shall hire
a skip and buy a shredder. I may even tidy up my computer,
delete old emails and files I don't need. Then I'll thin out the
books and reorganise the ones that are left according to
author and subject-matter, not shape and size, so that I may
at last be able to find a book when I want it.

But I am suddenly reminded of what happened to a
learned old friend, who employed some students to help
him sort out his books when he was moving house and
needed to halve his library. It was a long, slow, careful business, separating the precious and necessary books from all
those old review copies and books he'd been given and could
manage without. The students made two piles and then
arrangements with the rubbish people at the town hall, who
came and – you've guessed, of course – they took the wrong
ones, the precious and necessary ones. Imagine the horror
of that. Just thinking about it is beginning to discourage me
from my book cull.

And then there is all that paper. Teaching notes, lectures,
drafts of students' PhDs and completed ones in hard blue
covers. Stacks of references for students applying for jobs.
There are decades' worth of payslips, bank and royalty state-
ments (full of minuses and minuscule sums) waiting dustily
for a summons from the Inland Revenue to demonstrate my
honesty. In my part of London we have transparent pink
plastic recycling bags for paper. They will be filled with heaps
of theatre and concert programmes and exhibition notes. I
don't want them, and can't imagine why I've kept them. Is

it in order to prove that I've done these things, seen them, been alive? I go on believing that I might need them for something one day. Will there really come a day when I have nothing better to do than reread programmes of plays and concerts I went to twenty, thirty years ago? There are ancient biscuit tins full of letters from my mother and from friends. There is even a cupboard filled with the notebooks and files my children left here many years ago, when they'd finished university. And their school reports. One I found the other day contained that hopeless old chestnut about one of them not achieving what they were capable of, not reaching their potential. Rather like accusing someone of having a low pain threshold, it seems to me. How do you know what someone is capable of if they have doggedly refused to exhibit it?

If I work my way through all this dross I will start remembering and I'll probably never stop, and then I'll fail absolutely to throw anything away. I have a wise and efficient friend who tells me how to deal with these things as we stand under the showers after swimming. As she rings home on her mobile, she reminds me of those paintings of Mme Bonnard, impatiently posing for her husband while her bath water gets cold. No bill or bank statement needs to be kept for longer than three years, she tells me. Mine go back into the mists of time. They will be jettisoned. My bookshelves will contain so few books that those that are left will be able to lean amicably against one another like idle young men against a lamppost, and I will be able to insert new ones into appropriate places. I picture my drawers, my wardrobe, almost empty. Just a lavender bag or two and a mothball.

Hundreds of empty coat-hangers. I shall keep just enough in the way of clothes to cover myself, retain a modicum of decency, warmth, no more. There will be a short, neat row of shoes below, all in their pairs, with a shoe tree in each one of them. Nothing will be kept that I haven't worn at least once during the last year. Oh, I will do such things. My life will acquire the clearest, cleanest, simplest of lines. I might feel moved to invite a photographer in to see and record my new minimalist way of life. There'll be no clutter, nothing crazy. A perfect setting for the next stage of my life, whatever it is.

11

Dying

He died on one of those sinister, dark days between Christmas and New Year: days reserved, it sometimes seems, for events of exactly that sort. It was probably on Boxing Day. The swimming-pool reopened the day after, and I noticed on my way there that his encampment by the Fire Station was just as it usually was, though I couldn't see him in it. By the time, half an hour later, that I had had my swim and was walking home, everything had gone: mattress, duvets, deck chairs, plastic bags. And on the next day there was a notice on the wall saying that anyone who wanted to know what had happened to Paul should ask at the Methodist church opposite Habitat. I pushed through the glass doors which are meant to make you think you're going into a shop or a restaurant rather than a church, but I could find no one there to ask. The women at the pool knew nothing either, though each of them had stories to tell. One remembered him sitting happily in front of a television screen, doing something interactive with a video camera; another thought he'd looked yellow recently and had certainly made a terrible mess of the street. Another supposed that drink had been at the bottom of it. None of us knew him as Paul. I thought of him as my rough sleeper, RS for short. On the day after that a small and spreading shrine appeared outside the Fire Station: slim bunches of flowers in brown paper or cellophane, dozens of coloured night-lights, an empty champagne bottle, a crucifix made of twigs, a golden angel. There were messages, written in chalk on the brick wall and on the pavement, but also in pencil on scraps of paper. Three days later and the shrine was beginning to take up more space on the pavement than *he* had done, though there was evidence of a tidying hand at work.

I first saw him there, ensconced and proprietorial, about five years ago. It was a warm day in early September, just after the summer holidays. He had a long black beard, small bright black eyes and a red knitted hat with a badge on it. Though his eyes shone, they were also a little puffy at the edges. He seemed neat and organised, though, and he had the business of sleeping rough down to a fine art. He had trodden flat the backs of his small, shapely black shoes, making them easier to slip on and off, and his suitcase had clearly been sat on and crushed; but he folded his blankets on it during the day, and sat comfortably cross-legged beside them. I was never allowed to wonder whether he was cold or wet or fed up. He'd found the perfect place, he believed, and it was now his home: the wall behind him was always warm, he insisted surprisingly, because of the Fire Station,

and the concrete shelf above him, its two-metre depth sup-
ported by pillars to form a Brutalist arcade, protected him,
he assured me, from snow and rain and sun. He looked clean
in those days, and I wanted to ask him where he washed. I
thought he'd be offended by such a question, though, so I
never did. He smoked sometimes in the morning and had a
can of Special Brew at lunchtime. But I never saw him eat.

At first I stopped to talk to him every morning, though
not when he was talking to someone else, and he often was.
I didn't always want to stop, as I had to bend double to hear
him and be heard: the traffic was deafening. But he came to
expect it. Usually he praised Allah a lot, and the weather,
whatever it was like, but sometimes he was angry. Some boys
poured acid on his right hand, and he had to have it treated
in the hospital. That made for several kinds of lost ground for
a bit. He cursed the boys, though sparingly under the cir-
cumstances, and he wore a glove on that hand for several
weeks. Once a man spat at him, calling him a dirty foreigner
and a sponger, and the man was instantly hit by a fast-moving
car at the lights in front of the Fire Station. RS described the
satisfying parabola made by the man's body as he was flung
high into the air. Dead as a doornail by the time he hit the
ground, said RS, and his gesturing hands implied that fate
and the laws of revenge move in mysterious if also com-
fortingly predictable ways.

'Have I ever begged from you?' he asked me then, and he
hadn't. Indeed, I never managed to get him to accept more
than an occasional banana and a bar of chocolate. Sighing the
sigh of a man oppressed by abundance, he once forced on me

a Waitrose bag full of organic bread and rolls he'd been given and didn't want. He was often exasperated by gifts of blankets, pillows, mattresses, since they attracted police attention and criticism of him as a vagrant, a tramp, spoiling the beauty and the poshness (his word, spoken with resentment) of this Chelsea street. But there were gifts he kept: two deckchairs for his votaries and an unusually furry travelling rug. I was always conscious of an impregnable dignity, which dictated precisely what he would and wouldn't talk about, and I was economical with my questions as a result. He'd come to London long ago from Cyprus, the Turkish part of it, and he'd once worked, he said, in the catering department of the BBC, where he'd been promoted from the kitchen to management. We never got close to discussing what had taken him from the BBC to his domain outside the Fire Station.

I found Mr Brill one day at the top of a ladder cleaning someone's window, and I called up to ask him if he'd clean mine. That was years ago, and ever since then he has telephoned me every three months or so, loudly and lugubriously announcing himself with the words, 'Mr Brill here.' He dresses in elegant Mediterranean fisherman's gear, and his hair is carelessly styled in corn-coloured ringlets, their gleam sometimes heightened by a pinkish rinse. He has stories to tell about a depressed young wife, silent and sullen, of a daughter, a businesswoman, who has made a fortune she doesn't choose to share with him, of a brother who wrote a book about converting a French house, published it himself and sold a million copies, before dying inconveniently in

Bangkok. He is a little contemptuous of those who write books and do less well than his brother, and he doesn't read books himself, he tells me sternly, as if I might wish to press one on him. One day our conversation turned to the Rough Sleeper by the Fire Station. Mr Brill had spotted me talking to him as he bicycled by. He had known RS years ago, it turned out, when he was the smart young manager of a Bayswater hotel frequented by Mr Brill – in what capacity he did not divulge. RS had been married then, to a woman from Malta, and they had a baby daughter. But then he had vanished in a puff of smoke. There had been talk of an accident, Mr Brill said, of a child scalded to death in a hot bath and of guilt and grief so intense that both her young parents went mad. That was all. And there he sat now, calmly and comfortably settled halfway down the King's Road, as if that's where he'd always been and expected to be.

I went back to the church today, but they don't know much. 'Natural causes' is about all they can tell me, and that he was forty-one years old at the most. The 'Homeless Team' is dealing with the arrangements and the next of kin, and more information will be posted on the glass doors. I return to the shrine. A girl is kneeling on the pavement, adjusting the flowers. She looks up at me with tears in her eyes. A smartly dressed man asks me what happened, and I tell him what I know. I read the latest messages. One is from a woman who never met him, but used to wonder, as she looked down on him twice each day from the upper deck of the 319 bus, what drew people to this small man who seemed to be holding court beneath the concrete arches. 'King of Kings' is chalked up on the wall now, and 'You were the legend of the King's Road'. Someone called Olga thanks him in her letter for all the encouragement he gave her. He is congratulated by others on the place he has gone to and the company he now keeps. Someone jokily lays claim to his spot by the Fire Station and surrounds the message with a heart. There is a strongly Christian tone to it all, though one message reads 'Hallah' and is signed Akbar. His name is variously written as 'Paul' and 'Pablos' and 'Paulus', but clearly there are devotees who never knew his name, as I didn't.

One day two years ago, he was reading a book about Tutankhamun that someone had given him. It was when I asked him what he thought of it that he told me about Cyprus and then about the BBC. I don't think he could keep his mind on that book or any other; the street was always more interesting. Later I plucked up courage to mention our mutual friend, Mr Brill.

'What a silly billy that man is,' RS replied. 'He used to have three cars, and now he goes up and down the King's Road on a push-bike with a ladder on his shoulder. The man has three houses, you know, two in the country and one somewhere round here. Well, life goes up and down for all of us, doesn't it, up and down, up and down, like his ladder.'

He hated the heat, he told me, but he grandly refused to adapt his clothing to summer or winter. He was never without a hat, except once, after the acid incident, when he was peremptorily returned by the hospital to his patch, with no beard and a shaven head. But he had acquired a new hat by the following day. Someone gave him a blue baseball cap, a summer replacement for his dirty, faded winter one, and then a dull pink woollen one. I noticed him once as he contemplated himself in a window of the Fire Station: quite approvingly, I thought. If I went swimming really early I sometimes caught him walking round the tiny Dovehouse Green nearby. He told me once that he did two hundred press-ups there in the very early mornings. But he couldn't leave his things for long, he said, so sitting in the shade on a seat under a tree was a luxury he couldn't afford.

We hadn't spoken for a year or so before he died. He had told me again that story about the offending racist, and about the friendly God who arranged a fatal collision at the traffic lights. Only this time the offender was a woman wearing a fur coat and the car was a silvery Porsche, perhaps literally sent from heaven. And this time he elaborated further. God sees us all, the rich and the humble, him, me, all the flotsam on the King's Road. He licked his index finger and rubbed it against the brick wall behind him as he said these things. I felt foolish listening to him, ashamed of my gullibility the last time I had heard the tale, suddenly squeamish. And so I took to walking on the other side of the road, though we always waved at each other when there was a break in the traffic and pointed towards the sun, the sky, the rain, in ways which suggested contentment with these things, or the opposite.

I couldn't compete with his expanding court. There were not only those who sat down by him for chats during the day – one man wore a long black coat and had bright red eyes – there were some who joined him at night. A tousled woman emerged one morning from the pile of bedding next to his along the wall. It became a kind of dormitory. And in the daytime he and his friends talked and smoked and drank from cans of Special Brew. He sat in their midst; their leader and focus point, the still, listening and passive centre of it all. When he was alone he seemed older, fidgety. I saw him sometimes picking things from his beard and then sweeping them irritably from his coat. He was sometimes so engrossed in this that he didn't look up or notice my waving to him. And then he was more often still asleep in the morning when I went by, hung over, I imagined, making only the slightest hump in his mound of bedding; and when I caught him walking somewhere he no longer seemed youthful or agile. His legs were stiff and bent: I suppose from sitting cross-legged on the ground for most of his waking hours.

It poured with rain yesterday, and today the shrine has gone, as if washed away. There are printed notices, red on white, in the windows of the Fire Station: 'Rough sleepers will be moved on.' There were always people who wanted him moved on, but he resisted them. The notice on the church door announces a memorial service to be held at 12.30 next Wednesday in front of the Fire Station. The local minister will preside and the letters left at the place where he died will be read aloud.

There were at least fifty people there, and for the first time I looked out on the street as he had done. Across the road, on the other side of the traffic lights, stand the oldest, the most beautiful houses in Chelsea. One woman talked loudly of compassion and how little of it was around these days, as if we were to take credit for his life and his death and for being there at his send-off, and a rosy young man held his bike as he read the poem he'd written. A tall, striding madman I often see in the neighbourhood delivered an inaudible speech to the wall behind us, and two women from Social Services read some letters left at the shrine by strangers. The minister spoke of us all as brothers and sisters, but there were no 'next of kin', no 'loved ones'; only a curiously steely sense of shared admiration mingled with shame and puzzlement.

Today was cold and sunny as I walked past his old patch, the hemmed-in strip of Chelsea sky a rich, unspeckled blue. Last year, a car really did crash into the ancient garden walls in front of those beautiful early-eighteenth-century houses my rough-sleeping friend contemplated day and night, perhaps dreaming of revenge. The outside street walls were completely demolished and are now being rebuilt. Part of the covered way on the other side of the road, his side, where he lived, is boxed in with plywood now, to deter imitators, and the sign warning that 'rough sleepers' will be moved on is still there, curled and yellowing.

Studs Terkel's collection of witnesses to death, *Will the Circle Be Unbroken? Reflections on Death and Dignity*, a book he published in his late eighties, starts from the undertakers, the paramedics, the nurses and doctors and firemen and policemen, who encounter death daily and have to deal with sights and situations most of us spend our lives avoiding. To them, the death of an old person comes close to being a relief and

a pleasure, the end point of what one paramedic calls 'a natural progression', even if it has been a lonely death that went
undiscovered for several days. I am reminded of Charley, in
Henry Green's novel *Back*, who returns from the last war
minus a leg, and has 'a sort of holy regard for death in bed,
whereas dying out of doors meant damn all to him'. Death,
for people who work in jobs like those Terkel investigates,
is mostly wasteful and violent: something that happens
to the young through stabbings, shootings, car crashes, lives
'cut short'. These death professionals describe the bodies
they've retrieved and delivered to hospitals and morgues
in cool, horrifying detail. Yet when it comes to their own
deaths, of course, they are as mystified as the rest of us are
and as struck by grief when death confronts them, unable
to make use of what they've learned from their elaborate
professional encounters with dead bodies and blood and
agony when the business of dying glides inexorably towards
them and their friends and families.

One surgeon, used to emergencies and to conveying the
worst of news to relations and friends, insists that there is
'not a very firm line; there's a gradual blending from where
you're alive to where you're dead'. Most people, I dare say,
are more confident about knowing the difference, and would
say, as King Lear does of Cordelia, 'I know when one is dead,
and when one lives. She's dead as earth.' We were not so
sure when my mother died in her sleep on her ninety-second
birthday. My sister whipped off her bedclothes for a second
to check. Her limbs, which had become thin and childlike,
were spread out like a starfish. The undertaker collected her

the following day in a white van with wooden trays slotted
across its interior like an old-fashioned baker's. That was a
bad moment, the one when she became an entirely dead
person for me, something you had to dispose of in order to
be able to think about her again properly as she had been as
an alive person. Yet for several years she and the rest of the
family had been somewhat preoccupied with the delin-
quencies of that body.

That's what funerals are for, I suppose, to tide us over that
impossible transition. The dead person is there in a box to
remind you, just at the point when you start singing and
talking about their once manifold virtues and charms before
they were put in the box. The shocking absence is announced
by the bizarre presence of a dead body or by the ashes a dead
body has been reduced to. Seamus Heaney has written that
'memorial services are different from funerals. Funerals are
closer to the bones, as it were; they have to deal with the
rent in the fabric.'

No funeral ceremony can quite disguise the fact that
you're disposing of a person's body, their remains. That
person, however gloriously friends and family crack on about
them, is being disposed of. But how my mother and the
others would have loved to hear what comes next (and how
good we all get at the past conditional): the love, the praise,
the regret, the sorrow, the achievements, the uniqueness. My
mother longed and longed for compliments. She was insa-
tiable and she never got enough. I once imagined setting up
a Ministry of Compliments, in which high-flying civil servants would conscientiously conduct their researches into the

life of every single citizen, so that we could each of us count
on at least one really good and convincing compliment a year.
After all, they do it for our taxes, so why not for our conceit,
or even for that horrible thing, our dignity? When you think
how many compliments some people receive, and how 'dis-
proportionate', as people insist on saying these days, and
hyperbolic, some funerals can be, it doesn't seem much to
ask. My mother needed more than one a year, of course, as
we all do. But suddenly now that she was dead and no longer
in need of them there was an obituary singing her praises,
and a funeral, a summer one amid garish flowers in a garden
of remembrance, where all manner of people were warm
and affectionate and admiring. Gone were our memories of
crossness and eccentricity. We even found someone to recite
the Kaddish, and there was a party in my mother's garden
afterwards, and later on several exhibitions of her paintings
and prints.

You become a connoisseur of funerals and memorial services in old age, of sermons and orations and eulogies and
encomia and readings, of the music and the flowers and,
of course, the attendance. Then there are the gatherings
afterwards, the sandwiches and the tea and the wine, the
strangers who turn up, and the absences. All that in order
to blot out, just for a moment, the main absence, which may
make itself felt even more vividly after the funeral, when
everyone's gone home and there are only letters to write,
bills to pay and glasses to wash up. At some of these occasions you notice above all the exuberance of the celebration,
the exaggeration, the competitiveness.

At one service I went to, the dead man's daughter led us all in singing a round she'd composed on her father's name. The vast interior of that London church was filled with our uncertain singing to a gigantic photograph of the dead man over the altar, in the place where in Italy you'd expect to see a painting of the Ascension or the Crucifixion. At another, a pale, youngish and unconfident South African woman, efficient and unsmiling, was seen off as a heroine of the African National Congress, with pall-bearers and banners and draped flags galore. These, our old colleagues and friends and relations, must have been, it seems, the cleverest, the most remarkable, the most talented and the most charming of human beings. Why did we forget to remind them of all this when they lived, sometimes rather uncomfortably, among us? One old friend was photographed on her deathbed with her husband and daughter kneeling devotedly beside her dead body, and the photograph appeared in at least one national newspaper. Another old friend died in Greece, where cremations are not allowed, so that his body was flown to Bulgaria for incineration and back in time for his Athens funeral.

Some people organise their own funerals or memorial services. A quite young woman I once knew summoned an undertaker to her hospital bedside to give him her instructions for a funeral. He was about to leave when, finally, he put the question he'd held back from asking at the beginning: 'And who, might I ask, is the deceased?' 'The deceased will be myself,' she replied. Another old friend organised the readings and music for his memorial service and forbade all eulogies or, indeed, mentions of himself. Another had only music. The best funerals are full of stories. Then there are the men and women of the cloth, and the so-called 'Humanist' officiators, and all those professional ser-monisers who never met the deceased but have mugged up on them more or less aptly. That can be painful, though I enjoy imagining someone filleting out the essentials for them and the notes that were made and the pictures that were formed.

I once spent a mournful ten minutes at the wrong person's graveside. Lulled by what I took to be the Latin Mass, but which turned out to be Soho Italian, I took some time to realise my mistake and hotfoot it across that capa-cious and multicultural London cemetery to the graveside of the 105-year-old woman whose funeral I was meant to be at. I have been at the heartbreaking funerals of the very young and at the more ambiguous funerals of the terminally irri-table: people who wanted to put people in their place and to take a stand right up to the last moment. George Melly had a fine funeral that you felt he would certainly have enjoyed and should have been enjoying, in his brightly painted card-board coffin, flanked by a procession of old jazz players, while his very small granddaughter examined the shoes of the congregation and the coffin of her grandfather with studied care.

We all sidle up to the fact of death and then retreat, looking at our own shoes perhaps, not knowing even what it is that we don't know and want to know. Funerals remind us that we have only one go at a life and that this is the

beginning of an eternal absence. Dying may be even harder
for us to understand. A visit from his dying brother reminds
Levin in *Anna Karenina* of his own death: 'Just when the
question of how to live had become a little clearer to him,
a new insoluble problem presented itself – Death.' Some
months later, as he watches Nikolai actually on his deathbed,
he is shocked at how little he feels for this 'beloved' brother,
how impatient he is for it all to end. 'If he had any feeling left
for him it was more like envy of that knowledge which the
dying man now possessed and which he could not share.'
The sense that the dying, and perhaps even the dead, have
something to tell us is crucial to many people's thoughts
about death. Joan Didion has written of her disorientation
during the year following her husband's death, how she kept
his shoes just in case he came back after all. She is quite a
long way into her year of grief (or 'magical thinking', as she
puts it) when she asks herself, 'If the dead were truly to
come back, what would they come back knowing? Would
we face them? We who allowed them to die?' Accepting that
someone really has died can feel like letting them down, a
betrayal, leaving them to drop to the depths when they can
no longer hold on to you or to the cliff edge by their finger-
nails. We have let them be swept out of the life we are here
comfortably getting on with.

The need to know what it is impossible to know about
being dead may be at the root of religion, literature, legend,
magic. From the Orpheus story to the Resurrection to
experiences of reincarnation and ancestor worship, from vis-
itations to table-tapping, human beings can seem obsessed

with inventing and imagining the business of not being here, of ceasing to be who and what we are, of ghosts, of revenants, while looking at the same time for confirmation or enlightenment from those who are already dead. It is not necessarily that such stories comfort us or make the prospect of our own deaths any easier, and religions often have more to say about what to do than what to believe, let alone what is true. Levin is sure that Kitty understands something about death that he doesn't, because she knows how to treat her dying brother-in-law, how to be with him. She is neither horrified, nor silenced, as Levin is. For Kitty, Nikolai is quite simply a human being in particular need of help and friendship, and still alive; and her husband, perhaps mistakenly, attributes this to her religion rather than to her intelligence and humanity.

Our own absence from the world is certainly hard to imagine – perhaps it is beyond imagining – but many people are helped to imagine it by seeing their lives within a narrative that encompasses birth and death and the meanderings in between. Seamus Heaney has written about the place of Catholicism in his mother's life:

> There she was, doomed to biology, a regime without birth control, nothing but parturition and potato-peeling *in saecula saeculorum*, and the way she faced it and, in the end, outfaced it was by prayer and sublimation, toiling on in the faith that a reward was being laid up in heaven. She didn't have any simple-minded trust in this but went with the fiction of it, as it were, lived it as a wager rather than

an insurance. It was defiance as much as devotion . . .
Anyhow, the whole theology of suffering, the centrality
of sacrifice, of the cross, of losing your life to save it, all
that fitted in with what I saw in her.

We all go 'with the fiction of it' to some extent, and they will
be different fictions. Seamus Heaney wrote to me some
years ago as he was recovering from a stroke and I, more
prosaically, from my second knee replacement, in response
to something I had written about old age and dying and in
answer to a query I had put to his daughter about how her
father was managing old age. He was surprised, I think, by
my surprise, by my comparatively untethered skirmishes
with old age and thoughts of dying, and he counterposed his
own lifelong experience of the fiction that spoke to his
mother and to his young and now his older self, and he later
included parts of his letter in the autobiographical interviews
that make up his book, *Stepping Stones*:

> When I was young, from first awareness until at least the
> early teens, I dwelt in the womb of religion. My con-
> sciousness was formed, maybe better say dominated, by
> Catholic conceptions, formulations, pedagogies, prayers
> and practices. All kinds of simplifications of these matters
> coexisted with the canonical expression of all kinds of
> orthodox doctrine . . . So the drama of last things, nay
> the melodrama and terror of them were there from the
> start. You'd hardly got out of the cot, yet already you were
> envisaging the death bed.

And then there was a questioning of it all and later a kind of return:

> All this (which I don't think a great exaggeration of what was going on) seems to me to have provided a primal ordering, a structured reading of the mortal condition that I've never quite deconstructed. No doubt I might have talked differently, certainly more diffidently if you'd asked me about these matters thirty years ago. Naturally I went on to school myself as best I could from catechised youth into secular adult. The study of literature, the discovery of wine, women and song, the arrival of poetry, then marriage and family, plus a general, generational assent to the proposition that God is dead, all that cloaked and draped out the first visionary world. And yet in maturity, my growing familiarity with the myths of the classical world (and Dante's *Commedia* – Irish Catholic subculture with high cultural ratification) provided an imaginary cosmology that corresponded well enough to the original: poetic imagination proffering a world of life and a world of dark, a shadow world, not so much an afterlife as an after-image of life.

What fictions do we have, we Godless ones? Many of Terkel's witnesses look to their achievements in life, to their children, to what will be left of them when they die. 'Failure' and the death of children are their 'hell' on earth; a heartbroken circle of bereft friends and family, glimmerings of at least local fame, a sense of having done something well, their

only sight of a heaven thereafter. Would my Rough Sleeper
have been gratified, I wonder, by the scatter-gun effect of his
death on strangers? Terkel ends his collection with a miscellany of what may be thought of as extreme cases. There
is, for instance, the actress Uta Hagen, who thinks constantly
about death and who, at eighty-one, had never seen a dead
body and never meant to. There is a doctor who has worked
in several parts of East Africa amid torrents of deaths from
Aids and cholera and TB, and who despairs of communicat-
ing even a fraction of what he knows to people living as,
presumably, Uta Hagen and most of us live, protected from
the sheer scale and ordinariness of death. And there is the
ageing Chicago undertaker, who has embalmed most of his
family and looks forward to his son doing a 'beautiful job' on
him. He thinks of himself as a redeemer, who has organised
the funerals of innumerable murder victims and 'unclaimed
bodies':

They all went out of here fully dressed, and most of
them in tuxedos. When the tuxedos went out of style, a
friend brought me in a whole carload of them. So when
they had nothing, indigent – veterans that we got out of
the TB sanitarium or the VA hospital – they would send
them over to me and I would bury them for Veteran's
and Social Security . . . I put them all in tuxedos. People
would say: 'I thought he was penniless, I didn't think he
had any money.' I said, 'I took care of it.' I gave him suit,
shirt, tie, underwear, everything. They went out first
class.

A character in a recent Anne Tyler novel sees a sign above the doorway of a Mission for Indigent Men, and wonders whether 'indigent men know the word "indigent"'. It's difficult to be entirely convinced by the idea of Death the Leveller.

I watched my father die. I've lived ever since with the uncomfortable thought that if I didn't actually cause his death I certainly hastened it, accidentally dispatching him into eternity. He had been ill for six months or so, oddly and unusually ill and angrily cast down by this unspecific debility. It was as if he wanted to die and was encouraging his body to fail him in any way it saw fit. He was passed from hospital to hospital and landed finally in a small local one, which appeared to specialise in dying. There, he was given a small room to himself with a door leading into a garden. He could have gone home to his wife, to my mother, but he firmly dismissed any thought of this, feeling, I suspect, that he couldn't deal with what would be determined and most likely unsatisfactory attempts on her part to look after him. He was eighty-eight and she was about five years younger. I had been teaching in Montreal that summer, and there were worried phone calls. Should I cut short my stay and go home? He might die before I got back. But I didn't leave early and he didn't die, and there was time when I got back to London to visit him more than once. The weather was hot and clammy, I remember, and the door from his room to the garden was left open. He sat rigidly and somehow furiously in an uncomfortable hospital chair with his back to the garden, refusing even to look out of the window or the door, and spitting out information about what was going on in the various remnants of the old Yugoslavia: his usual lecturing style, but more impatient and exasperated than ever now with the world's ignorance, and mine.

I was summoned late one morning by one of my sisters, who was already at my father's bedside with my mother. It looked as though he was really dying. As I drove to the hospital, I imagined what this would mean and what I'd find, and I could hear the hoarse rasping noise his breathing made even before I had reached the open door to his room. An unsmiling nurse grabbed my arm as I went in, inviting me to call her at once if he seemed to get worse, muttering her readiness if that happened to administer TLC – an acronym I'd not heard used before. An hour or two later, and I could hardly bear the exhausted, straining efforts he made to breathe, the stuffy room, the three of us alternately, helplessly, mopping his brow and holding his hands. So I went out to find the nurse and told her that he seemed to be suffering more than he should be. Could she do something? She was back in a flash with her syringe. He died instantly, perhaps killed by whatever she had injected into him or perhaps from the shock of it. I'd imagined that she'd bring solace, relief of some sort, not death. Those letters, TLC, and the 'tender loving care' they stand for, have seemed murderous to me since. As soon as he was dead, my father became about three-quarters of his usual size. He didn't shrivel. His face remained smooth and yellowish. But it was smaller, shrunk, and his handsome nose became a little beak. We summoned

other members of the family. The door into the garden was
left open, and we all sat out on the lawn in the sun, and every
so often one of us would go back into his room to look at
him. It was almost as if we thought he might get up and leave
if we didn't check on him from time to time. I didn't want
to see him again. That strange effigy frightened me. But
something – shame, curiosity, politeness – made me do so
several times, frightening myself as I looked at that strange
waxwork on the bed. I found it difficult touching his cold
hand, but I made myself do it. The nails were the same nails,
but everything else was changed.

Years earlier, when my father-in-law died, my husband,
as inexperienced about death as we are when we're first
confronted with it and as we go on being, consented to
having the coffin left open and placed in our tiny back
basement room, to which we had no key. This had, I think,
been offered as a popular and even admirable option. I
didn't sleep that night, for fear that my small son might
wander into the room where his grandfather lay in his
coffin, made up like a doll, wholly unrecognisable, and, to
me, as I assumed he would be to a child, utterly terrifying.
Perhaps one reason why I am not afraid of my own death
is that I know I won't have to see or deal with my own
dead body.

Tonight, I believe, there is to be a programme shown
on television in which we may watch as an 'assisted suicide'
is performed in Switzerland. The day's news has rung
with disagreements about whether this – the suicide and the
programme about it – is a good thing or not. Montaigne

might have approved of the debate, at least. He thought and wrote about death throughout his life, and frequently advised himself about ways of dealing with its terrors and its imminence:

> Let us deprive death of its strangeness; let us frequent it, let us get used to it; let us have nothing more often in mind than death. At every instant let us evoke it in our imagination under all its aspects. Whenever a horse stumbles, a tile falls or a pin pricks however slightly, let us at once chew over this thought: 'Supposing that was death itself?'

Montaigne could write confidently of death's imminence in his thirties and live on to be an old man by the standards of the time. We, who constantly witness violent death on television, real death as well as counterfeit, also expect to avoid it, if not for ever, then for many more years than people did in the past. Even the peaceful death of the very old is greeted as in some sense shocking, and probably avoidable. Death continues to be simultaneously ordinary and extraordinary, a part of life and the end of the world.

Or as Turgenev has Bazarov say on his deathbed at the end of *Fathers and Sons*, 'It's an old joke, death, but it's new for each one of us.'

Acknowledgements

Old age has been my time for friends, and I owe more friends more than I can ever acknowledge. Several of them have generously read chapters and encouraged and helped me and given me ideas throughout the writing of this book. Listing them in alphabetical order hardly represents the gratitude I feel towards each of them, but there it is. They are Deanne and Joe Bogdan, Deborah Britzman, Anne Bromwich, Carmen Callil, Joanna Cummins, Michael Holroyd, Diana Melly, Rachel and Jonathan Miller, Andrew O'Hagan, Ursula Owen, Alice Pitt, Naomi Roberts, Mary Taubman, Emma Tennant, Anne Turvey and John Yandell.

Karl Miller has given me more than encouragement. His company has made the experience of old age interesting, tolerable and even amusing. The same could be said for Daniel, Sam and Georgia Miller. The late Richard Poirier, Stephanie Volmer and Jackson Lears of *Raritan* in America have published versions of most of these chapters in their magazine over the last three or four years. I am hugely grateful to them for that, and I thank them; as I thank Lennie Goodings, Viv Redman and Virago, for publishing my book at such a cold and stony time for publishers.

In addition, I want to thank Judy and the late David Drew; and William Salaman and Joanna Wright for allowing me to print unpublished material they had shown me. I also thank Margaret Atwood and Virago for letting me quote from her novel *Cat's Eye*; John Berger and Penguin Press for allowing me to quote from his *Ways of Seeing*; J. M. Coetzee and Harvill & Secker for permission to quote from his *Diary of a Bad Year*; William Dalrymple for permission to quote from his *Nine Lives: In Search of the Sacred in Modern India*; Seamus Heaney for permission to quote from a letter, and both him and Dennis O'Driscoll for permission to quote from their *Stepping Stones*. The quotations from Philip Roth's *Everyman*, published by Jonathan Cape, are reprinted by permission of The Random House Group Ltd. I thank Mariam Said, Michael Wood and the Wylie Agency for permission to quote from Edward W. Said, *On Late Style: Music and Literature Against the Grain* (Copyright © 2006. All rights reserved). Thanks also to Frederick Seidel and Faber & Faber for letting me print a verse from 'Climbing Everest', and to Hugo Williams for letting me quote from his article 'Freelancing', published in *The Times Literary Supplement* in 2006.

The translations of writing by Simone de Beauvoir and Fernande Olivier are mine, as are the translations of lines from Chekhov's *Uncle Vanya* and from Turgenev's *Fathers and Sons*. The translations of passages from Michel de Montaigne's *Complete Essays* are by M. A. Screech, and I would like to thank the Penguin Group for letting me use them here.

List of Books

Some of the books about old age and related topics that I read or reread while I was writing this book:

Kingsley Amis	*Ending Up* and *The Old Devils*
Diana Athill	*Somewhere Towards the End*
Julian Barnes	*The Lemon Table* and *Nothing to Be Frightened Of*
John Bayley	*Iris*
Simone de Beauvoir	*Old Age*
Saul Bellow	*Ravelstein*
Wayne Booth	*The Art of Growing Older. Writers on Living and Aging*
Louise Bourgeois	*Destruction of the Father. Reconstruction of the Father. Writings and Interviews 1923–1997*
Charlotte Brontë	*Villette*
Anton Chekhov	*Uncle Vanya* and *A Boring Story*
J. M. Coetzee	*Elizabeth Costello* and *Diary of a Bad Year*
William Dalrymple	*Nine Lives*
Jared Diamond	*Why is Sex Fun?*
Joan Didion	*The Year of Magical Thinking*
George Eliot	*Daniel Deronda*
Janice Galloway	*This Is Not About Me*
Simon Gray	*The Smoking Diaries* and *Coda*
Seamus Heaney and Dennis O'Driscoll	*Stepping Stones* (interviews with Seamus Heaney, by Dennis O'Driscoll)

Carolyn Heilbrun	*Writing a Woman's Life* and *The Last Gift of Time: Life Beyond Sixty*
Norah Hoult	*There Were No Windows*
Frank Kermode	*The Sense of an Ending*
Ian McEwan	*On Chesil Beach*
Michel de Montaigne	*The Complete Essays* (trans. M. A. Screech)
Frances Morris (ed.)	*Louise Bourgeois* catalogue, Tate Modern (contains essays by Linda Nochlin and Robert Storr)
Alice Munro	*Too Much Happiness*
Fernande Olivier	*Picasso and His Friends* (trans. Jane Miller)
Amos Oz	*A Tale of Love and Darkness*
Alexander Pushkin	*The Queen of Spades*
Dorothy Richardson	*Pilgrimage*
Samuel Richardson	*Clarissa*
David Rieff	*Swimming in a Sea of Death. A Son's Memoir*
Philip Roth	*Patrimony* and *Everyman*
Edward Said	*On Late Style*
Esther Salaman	*A Collection of Moments*
William Shakespeare	*King Lear*
Helen Small	*The Long Life*
Muriel Spark	*Memento Mori*
Studs Terkel	*Will the Circle Be Unbroken? Reflections on Death and Dignity*
Leo Tolstoy	*Anna Karenina* and *The Death of Ivan Ilyich*
Peter Townsend	*The Family Life of Old People. An Inquiry in East London*
Ivan Turgenev	*Fathers and Sons*
Anne Tyler	*Noah's Compass*
John Updike	The *Rabbit* novels and *Seek My Face*; 'Late Works. Writers and artists confronting the end' in the *New Yorker*, 7 August 2006
Sarah Waters	*The Night Watch*

Edith Wharton	*Ethan Frome*
Bernard Williams	'The Makropulos Case: Reflections on the Tedium of Immortality' in *Problems of the Self: Philosophical Papers 1956–1972*
Richard Wollheim	*Germs: A Memoir of Childhood*
Stefan Zweig	*Beware of Pity*

Index